ZARIFA

ZARIFA

A WOMAN'S BATTLE IN
A MAN'S WORLD

ZARIFA GHAFARI
&
HANNAH LUCINDA SMITH

PUBLICAFFAIRS

NEW YORK

PublicAffairs
Hachette Book Group
1290 Avenue of the Americas, New York, NY 10104
www.publicaffairsbooks.com
@Public_Affairs

Printed in the United States of America

Originally published in Great Britain in 2022 by Virago Press
First US Edition: October 2022

Published by PublicAffairs, an imprint of Perseus Books, LLC,
a subsidiary of Hachette Book Group, Inc. The PublicAffairs name and
logo is a trademark of the Hachette Book Group.

The Hachette Speakers Bureau provides a wide range of authors for
speaking events. To find out more, go to www.hachettespeakersbureau.com
or call (866) 376-6591.

The publisher is not responsible for websites (or their content)
that are not owned by the publisher.

Typeset in Bembo by M Rules

Library of Congress Control Number: 2022943385

ISBNs: 9781541702639 (hardcover), 9781541702653 (e-book)

LSC-C

Printing 1, 2022

For the brave women of Afghanistan,
who battle brutality and extremism
for freedom and humanity.

Prologue

February 2022

Changa, Wardak province

The men wanted to know everything about Germany. After the teenagers had cleared away the platters of rice and meat and half-finished bowls of milk pudding, folding up the orange plastic floor mat to catch the spilled grains and sugar wrappers inside, the elders fixed their eyes on me and listened in intent silence as they sipped their teas. I took a breath, fixed my headscarf, and started by telling them about the driving licences.

'You have to do hours of classes!' I told them. 'And then you have to take a test.'

They exchanged surprised glances. None of them had ever had their driving abilities assessed before they got behind the wheel. I ramped it up another notch.

'And then, they *take your licence away* if you break the rules too many times!'

Now they were really shocked. Germany was the land of freedom, wasn't it? So what did they mean by denying a man's right to drive? I hadn't even got on to the real stuff yet – the jaw-dropping price of potatoes in the supermarkets, the money you had to hand over to the government before you even saw your paycheque. I knew this would be stunning news to them, and that they wouldn't quite believe me. Here in Changa, a remote, rural village, sixty miles but eight hours by car on dirt tracks through the mountains from Kabul, it was assumed that anyone who had made it to Europe must be living a life of great luxury. And now here I was, the emissary from a promised land, a young Afghan woman, no less, telling them they had got it all wrong.

I could hardly blame these men: they had little else but hope. Changa was a collection of beige mud huts, with no running water or mains electricity. To get a phone signal you had to climb higher up the mountain. To go to the toilet, you had to squat in a hut on the hillside. School was a single-room madrassa for the boys, where Qurans and other religious literature were piled up along the walls next to huge heaps of prayer mats, and a courtyard classroom open to the elements. This is where the girls sat cross-legged on the ground for their lessons, when in February, the melting snowfall turned the hard-packed earth into mud. I would not have kept an animal there.

For the men, the imminent arrival of spring heralded an agreeable few months, when even those who believed Germany to be the land of Audis for all would proudly state that they preferred to stay in their village. In spring, the snow slides off the jagged mountains, revealing a layer of emerald-green grass, and new leaves on the bare branches of apple trees. The sun rises earlier and heats the earth a little deeper every day; within weeks, everything would bloom into a fragrant canopy, and the men would wade into the river at the bottom of the valley in loose shorts and T-shirts to splash water at each other and shriek with delight. The women would not join in. Almost all of them in Changa over the age of fourteen were married; for them, there was little time for play.

Most of the amenities in Changa, including the school, had been provided by the Taliban. In the twenty years that the international aid organisations and NATO armies had spent in Afghanistan, barely a penny of the billions of pounds that were poured into the country made it to villages like this one. They might not even have known that the regime in Kabul had changed in 2001 had it not been for the air strikes and night raids that came soon after. The last time foreigners had come to Changa was in the 1980s, when two French doctors dropped in – if you discounted the Americans who dropped from the skies with their parachutes and Robocop gear. Nobody had bothered to come and pave the road, or fund a market, or build a sewage system. The carcasses of Russian tanks remained by the roadside, rusting heaps turning the same ochre as the earth after thirty years. One Swedish aid organisation had funded a basic maternity clinic in the former school, and trained local women as midwives to assist with straightforward births. Otherwise, everything else here was provided by the Taliban's parallel state, from education to security and the Sharia legal system. One of the biggest buildings in the area, which had once belonged to a governor of Wardak, was now the militants' prison. And it was for that reason, as well as for their own protection, that everyone in the village supported the Taliban.

The curious old men of Changa, the fathers and supporters of those Talib boys, looked like a *National Geographic* stereotype of Afghanistan. Their turbans, elaborate rolls of pristine fabric, increased the diameter of their heads by half again. They wore huge woollen *pato*, shawls in earthy colours draped elegantly around their shoulders and necks. Outside, in the bitter mountain wind, they pulled the *pato* over their heads and wrapped them like a mask over their nose and mouth, and under their chins, exposing only their owlish amber eyes. Some teenagers adopted the style, adding a swoosh of kohl around their lashes for extra effect. They had gathered to greet me, inviting me to eat in the best salon of their homes, warmed by the family's sole gas-powered heater, all of us sitting comfortably on plump red cushions laid out around the edges of the room. The women were elsewhere, in a colder edge of the house, waiting for their turn to eat the food they had prepared for us all.

To an outside observer it may have seemed like nothing had changed in Changa for hundreds of years, that this was a place unmoved by the outside world's march towards modernity. But one small detail gave the truth away. Hung up high on the turquoise-painted wall, festooned with pink and yellow garlands, was a photograph of a young man with a pencil moustache and side-parted hair. The print had clearly been professionally taken decades ago, and Mohammad Jan, the man staring out at his turbaned descendants, was wearing a suit and tie. In the early 1970s, when the picture was taken, he had been a young traffic officer in Kabul, having left Changa to forge a new life in the capital. In Kabul, he had been seduced by leftist politics and its promise of a progressive, democratic Afghanistan. That led him to join the Khalq Party (People's Democratic Party), a socialist bloc with friendly ties to the Soviet Union. He married, started a family, and had no reason to believe that his life and theirs would not continue in this modern fashion.

But in 1973 everything started to unravel. First, King Zahir Shah was deposed in a coup led by his cousin, Lieutenant General Mohammad Daud Khan, who declared his relative 'corrupt and effete' and vowed to bring democracy to the country. General Khan installed the Khalq Party as the government and declared himself president. The Soviets then took advantage, and started ramping up their political influence. In 1978 a Moscow-backed communist faction launched its own coup, killed Khan, and took power. The new government was headed by Nur Muhammed Taraki, a leftist writer and journalist convinced of the need for a Bolshevik-style revolution. He immediately began seizing and redistributing private wealth, annihilating the bourgeoisie as the country descended into anarchy. Within a year, the brand-new government was riven by factional disputes, and in December 1979 the Soviet army crossed the border, reaching Kabul within days and installing its own puppet government, kickstarting the decade-long Soviet-Afghan war, with the resistance made up of religious men who called themselves the mujahideen, or holy warriors, for whom godless communism was an abomination.

Mohammad Jan was no longer a progressive: according to the mujahideen, he was a traitor. Back in Changa, support for the mujahideen's resistance was absolute. And so, like millions of Afghans, Mohammad opted for self-preservation. He shed his Western-style suit and tie, moved his young family back to his village, began working as a truck driver, and threw his support behind the mujahideen faction of Gulbuddin Hekmatyar, a brutal warlord and Islamic fanatic.

In the four decades since Mohammad returned to Changa, the regime in Afghanistan had changed three times, from Soviet puppet to Taliban theocracy, to internationally backed government, and finally back to the Taliban. In villages like this, however, the upheavals in Kabul meant little. They had supported the mujahideen, then they had supported the Taliban when it turned out to be the most powerful among the factions. In 2001, when the Taliban was ousted from Kabul and the other cities, its fighters retreated to the countryside – to places like Changa – and continued governing through a parallel state. Eventually, in August 2021, the Taliban's parallel state became Afghanistan's full state once again.

The men in the room, some of them the sons of Mohammad Jan and others his brothers, were largely happy that the Taliban was back in charge. The previous government of President Ashraf Ghani had been corrupt to the core, pocketing much of the international money that was meant to improve the lives of ordinary Afghans. Now, the villagers did not have to worry about night raids on their houses, or foreign soldiers storming into their houses with their dirty boots while their wives and daughters were at home. They hoped the new Taliban government might now spend some money on Changa.

Yet, in a land of paradoxes, the very least was this photo on the wall – of the most respected man in the family captured for eternity in his smart Western suit, his eyes full of hope for an Afghanistan in which women could be equal to men.

My name is Zarifa Ghafari. I am an Afghan woman, born in 1994 in the time of my country's civil war and raised during the Taliban's first regime. I came of age in the era following 2001, as a supposedly democratic government was being propped up by Western armies, aid organisations, and billions of dollars. As an adult, I became the first female mayor of Wardak province, a Taliban heartland west of Kabul. In that position I became one of the most prominent women in the country, and an outspoken opponent of the Taliban. For that, the militants tried to assassinate me three times, and when they failed to do that, they killed my father. When Afghanistan fell once again to the Taliban in August 2021, I was forced to flee, boarding one of the chaotic evacuation flights from Kabul airport to a new life as a refugee in Germany.

Six months later, I took a decision that made me a hero to some of my countrymen, and an apologist according to others: I returned to Afghanistan, determined to look the Taliban in the eye. Some people asked how I did it, and why. Practically, it was simple: I am still an Afghan citizen, after all. I went back on a plane, like anyone else.

Emotionally and physically it was difficult. In the months since they retook power, the Taliban had arrested several female activists and imposed a raft of rules restricting women's freedom. I worried that I would be arrested the moment I presented my passport at the immigration booth, or that a pumped-up young Talib at a checkpoint would recognise me and be unable to contain his rage.

In order to ensure my safety I secured the backing of the German government, and an assurance from the Taliban's leadership that nothing would happen to me while I was in Afghanistan. For that, I was accused by other Afghan activists of whitewashing the new regime. But I did not go for political reasons, nor did I hold any meetings or negotiations with the Taliban. I went to visit the humanitarian project that I set up in Kabul soon after my exile to Germany, and to show solidarity with the women still in Afghanistan. What I found in my country, the place I feared I might never be able to return to, was far more complex than the simple black-and-white narratives imposed onto it.

While I was mayor of Wardak, from May 2018 to June 2021, I would never have been able to go to Changa, even though it was, on paper, under my responsibility. Taliban territory started within a mile of my office in the provincial capital, Maidan Shahr, and even if I had escaped an ambush on the road I would certainly have been arrested in the village. In my time in office I watched the Taliban chip away government control over Wardak until, finally, the fight came into the city itself, forcing me to leave for a new government posting in Kabul. Yet now that the entire country had fallen to the Taliban, I was able to travel freely, and was welcomed by the village elders. On a crisp morning, as the early spring sunshine started melting the snow on the mountaintops, I distributed aid packages, and spoke with the villagers about their economic problems. The elders invited me into Changa's meeting hall for an audience – the first time any of them had sat and debated local politics with a woman. Huddled into the small room, underneath the white flag of the Taliban pinned on the wall, they explained why they were pleased that the old government was gone.

'Now there is no war, no bloodshed,' said one, whose turban gleamed white as the snow. 'Aid was previously going to the people connected with the warlords and powerful people. At least some now reaches the people in need.'

Another, a man with a face as crinkled and brown as a walnut, disagreed. 'But now the Taliban is distributing the aid to their own people,' he said. 'It's still not going to the people who really need it.'

For half an hour, I talked with these men who, only months ago, would have celebrated my death. I did not feel offence, or anger. The reasons for this are not easy to explain. The attempts on my life while I was mayor were not about me personally. They were about what I represented to them: a rotten government that had done nothing for ordinary Afghans, and a type of women's liberation that, in villages like Changa, was seen as a foreign imposition. For the Taliban, killing me would have been a victory, a way of reminding the government in Kabul that they were still in charge in places like Wardak. But now that the Taliban was victorious, they had lost their motivation for killing me. In fact, their needs were better served by protecting me. Desperate for international recognition, and the financial support that would come with it, in February 2022 the Taliban were on a public relations drive, trying to convince the world that they were a different group from the one that had ruled Afghanistan in the 1990s, the one that had banned TV and music and reduced women to walking shadows in blue burkas.

For most of my meeting with the elders, I was the one holding the floor. These men, most of whom would never heed the opinion of their wives, sisters or daughters, listened in spellbound silence. I have always been a natural at public speaking: even when I am dropping with fatigue I can flick a switch for an interviewer or an audience. It is a skill I started honing as a girl when I realised how effective it was; I have found it as useful when speaking with world leaders at glitzy conferences as it has been in meetings with illiterate Afghan men in modest mud huts.

'I am requesting – no, begging – you to let your daughters go to school. If the school here is rebuilt as a high school, you must allow them to study until twelfth grade,' I said.

'If you want to save yourselves from this misery, please educate your children and specifically your daughters. If you invest in your son's education, he will bring you money. But if you invest in your daughter's education, she will then educate her own children when she becomes a mother, and then her grandchildren. If you educate one woman, you are saving ten generations.'

The men – illiterate but wise – nodded their heads sagely, and at the end thanked me profusely for coming to see them. One by one, they shook my hand and filed out of the room. They all hoped that I might be able to change something in Changa, pleased that a politician, even a former one, had bothered to make the difficult journey to their village. They were all impressed by me, and by the path I had chosen for myself. Yet, had you asked any one of them whether they would have wanted their daughters to do something similar, their answers would have been unanimous: *Of course not. This is Afghanistan.*

The women of Changa wanted to talk about children: specifically, how many each of them had. In a place where women are barely allowed out of the house, where few are educated and even those rarely beyond primary school, the one way a woman can earn respect is through the number of children she gives birth to. Mahdia didn't know her own age, she could only guess. After marrying at thirteen, and with one child a year since then – with sixteen of twenty children surviving – she reckoned she was in her mid-thirties. She looked remarkably well, with smooth dark skin over high cheekbones, and a sparkle in her youthful eyes offset by the red of her embellished headscarf and the *sheen khal*, a small blue dot tattooed on her forehead used by some Afghans to ward off the evil eye. She felt blessed, she told me.

'This is just how life is for us,' Mahdia replied, when I asked how she could tolerate such an existence. 'We have never seen anything different to what we have. It just is.'

It crushed me to hear these words from one of my countrywomen. I had come here not for political purposes, nor personal promotion, but to find what I could salvage from my country now that the Taliban was back in charge.

Through my humanitarian foundation, Assistance and Promotion for Afghan Women, I had opened a women's training centre and maternity clinic in Kabul. But I knew that it was here, in places like Changa, that I had the possibility of sparking real change. I turned to the younger, unmarried women, and asked them to leave the room. I wanted to speak frankly, but I also knew that the older women would not thank me if I brought up taboo topics in front of their daughters. Once we were alone, I started talking about their right, and their responsibility, to limit their family numbers.

'Having one, two or three kids is normal,' I told them. 'But with every child you give birth to you are losing a huge amount of energy. Maybe it will take some years off your life. And if your child is a daughter, then one day your husband is going to come home and announce that he has found a man for her to marry. And just as it was for you, she is not going to have any choice in the matter.'

If life was tough for the men of Changa, for the women it was truly grim. Most men forbade their wives from seeing a male doctor, even when they were in labour and their lives in danger. Even if they did allow it, the visit would have meant an hours-long journey down those bumpy mountain tracks on the back of a motorbike, since few people here had cars. There were only a handful of women in the country who had been educated to a level that would have allowed them to become competent health workers. Most babies are born at home, yet Afghan women have one of the highest fertility rates in the world, with men usually making the decision of how many children their wives should have. As in many Islamic countries, children are seen as a mark of male virility and pride – the more children a man can have the better. In fact, pregnancy and childbirth has killed more women and children in Afghanistan over the past forty years than bullets and bombs ever did. Around one in ten women and one in twenty babies die during labour.

But in conservative societies, change can only happen gradually, through the generations.

'Listen to me,' I told the women. 'My mother had eight children. But I am not going to have more than two. And they will themselves have their own thoughts on this issue.'

I told them about how my family had struggled when I was a child, how some nights we had nothing to cook but plain rice. I described how my family's situation had changed when my mother was able to work again, how it had lifted us out of survival mode to a place where we could think of a better future. I told them how my father had been killed, and the struggles we were now going through as refugees. When they saw that I was not simply some rich woman, perhaps educated abroad and now coming back to tell Afghans how to live, they began to trust me. Little by little, the women started opening up, dropping the protective pretence that they were happy with everything life in Changa had handed them. By the end of our conversation, tears were rolling down Mahdia's face.

The next morning, before I set off back to Kabul, I ate breakfast with the same women and their daughters. We sat around the edges of the room that had seemed so bare and cold to me the night before, the floor now laid out with little plates of jam, eggs and cheese. The morning sun beamed through the window, lighting up a vista of snow-covered mountains outside. It was a joyous, gossipy meal. The women wished me well for my own marriage, and said they would pray for me to return to Changa soon.

'We are so proud of you, so happy you are here,' one told me. 'It is my wish that my daughter can rise up like you.'

If I had only changed the mind of that one woman, my long journey to Changa had been worth it.

One

If you lined up my mother, my grandmother and me side by side, all of us standing in profile, you would spot our blood tie straight away. All of us have the same aquiline nose that dominates our silhouettes. Many women in Asia opt for plastic surgery to change such a nose, reducing it to a stump of a ski slope diminished by their other bold features. I have never understood why they would do such a thing in pursuit of a Westernised form of femininity. For me, this trait I have inherited through my maternal bloodline is a mark of our strength.

To explain how I became an Afghan woman who fought back against her society, I have to start from the beginning. My whole family story has been shaped by Afghanistan's tragedy. Trauma has been passed down with my DNA.

My mother, Karima, was three when her father was murdered by one of the mujahideen militias that were busy carving up Afghanistan. It was 1980, a year after the Soviet army invaded, and the mujahideen had already decided that ethnicity was more important than country or faith. They splintered into ethnic factions: Pashtun, Hazara, Tajik, Uzbek. Most of Afghanistan's ethnic patchwork was fighting each other, each group led by a man who had spotted opportunity in turmoil. Gulbuddin Hekmatyar, leader of the Pashtun faction, was one who committed acts of barbarity in the name of religion. His chief henchman was Zerdad Faryadi, a thug who took his nickname from one of his bodyguards, who was reputed to engage in cannibalism. The guard was known as 'The Dog', and Faryadi as 'The Big Dog'. Their main concern was the Jalalabad border crossing into Pakistan, which had become an escape route for thousands of people, mostly liberals and intellectuals, who were trying to flee the escalating bloodshed. Faryadi and his dog controlled the border checkpoint, extorting money from people as they tried to leave.

But groups of all ethnicities committed atrocities – there were no good guys, only bad and worse. The Tajik leader was Ahmad Shah Masood, 'the Lion of Panjshir', who repelled seven Soviet offensives on his domains in the north of Afghanistan and would be assassinated by the Taliban two days before the attacks on the Twin Towers in 2001. The Hazara had Abdul Ali Mazari, later captured, tortured and killed, and his corpse flung from a helicopter. The Uzbek had Abdul Rashid Dostum, notorious for his lavish tastes, which included a bulletproof Cadillac, and his war crimes. Their militiamen, drunk on their sudden power, would roam the streets of the villages at night, searching for girls to rape. There was a gory urban legend told in Kunduz, the northern province where my mother spent her early years, of a woman who had the misfortune to get caught in a fight between two factions. The fighters came into her house as she was feeding her infant son, cut off her breasts and killed the boy. One favoured method of execution was the *raqs morda* – the death dance. The killers would cut off their victim's head, throw it into a vat of boiling oil, and laugh as the decapitated body twitched on the ground.

My maternal grandfather, Abdul Rahman Osmani, was the principal of a school in Kunduz. The school, which taught both boys and girls, was opened in the brief era when the socialist government made women's rights a key concern. In Kabul, bare-headed women attended university classes alongside men, some of the women wearing miniskirts as they walked to classes, their arms full of books. Still, they were anomalies. Alongside them in the Kabul streets were outraged men staring at their brazen displays of liberation, and other women wearing burkas. Most of the country remained deeply conservative, and in the villages women still went about shrouded in veils and long cloaks. But there was, at least, the beginnings of change.

After the invasion, the Soviet-backed government and army kept control of Kabul but the religious ideologues soon commanded power in the countryside. As they rose, any small gains that had been made for women screeched into reverse. According to the mujahideen, educating girls was sinful – that alone was my grandfather's crime. For years, he had lent his beautiful voice to the call to prayer that rang out from the local mosque five times a day. Yet the warlords, the so-called holy warriors, persecuted him. Tajik militiamen arrested him and held him in Sher Khan Bandar, a dank prison next to the Panj river, which marks

Afghanistan's border with Tajikistan. After forty days they led him into the Khwaja Ghar mountains, where they tied him with ropes to another prisoner and shot them both dead with one bullet. Then they threw their bodies into the nearby river, where my grandfather would remain. My mother's eldest brother was only seven years old, too young to take on the task of retrieving his father's corpse. There was no one my grandmother could take her case to – the warlords made the law. Soon after, my grandmother, a widow at twenty-seven, moved with her six children to Kabul.

They rented a small house in Deh Dana, a district in the far south of the city close to the neoclassical Darul Aman palace, surrounded by the Sher Darwaza mountain and the remains of Kabul's ancient city walls. Its name means 'the place of the educated' but by the 1980s it was turning from a middle-class area into a slum. Refugees flooded there as the warlords strengthened their grip on the countryside, swelling the genteel capital into unruly, overcrowded shambles. But tight communities formed in these urban hinterlands. New arrivals picked the neighbourhoods where others from their province had already settled, creating imperfect copies of their villages in the city. Later, in the 1990s when the Taliban came, most of the original, wealthier Kabulis left their homes in the rich inner districts, many of them emigrating to Europe and the United States. But these poorer immigrants into Kabul stayed.

Afghan mores dictate that my grandmother should have married one of her dead husband's brothers, accepting a reduced position as a second wife in return for economic security. But she chose the hard road, taking a job in a factory to feed her children as a single mother. It was the first time she had worked outside the home. From being the wife of a school principal, a respected woman in her village, she had become just another refugee among hundreds of thousands in the tough city. In my country, you can never take what you have for granted. Tomorrow, it might all be gone.

Family histories are made up of many tides, and some of them can turn for the better even as others turn for the worse. As the Soviet Union collapsed and the Berlin Wall fell, Kabul became one of the first victims of the Cold War hangover. The Soviet army withdrew from Afghanistan in 1989 – another great power humbled, but leaving a shattered society and much of the country as rubble. But in Kabul the war still felt a long way away. My mother went to school in the capital, and after classes went to collect the housekeys from my grandmother in the clothing factory, where she worked sewing uniforms for the Afghan army.

It was my father's sisters who first spotted my mother in 1991, when she was fourteen years old. My aunties were also working in the factory, and had their own family story of flight. My paternal grandparents had once lived in rare luxury. My grandfather, Faramoz Ghafari, was working with a German company in one of the development projects in Herat province. He was also a respected leader in his village and a hugely wealthy man. The family lived in a mansion in the countryside, three storeys high behind ornate iron gates. My grandmother, Bibi Rabia, lived like a queen with more than forty silk Afghani rugs to furnish her house, hand-stitched shoes and chests full of silver and gold jewellery, studded with precious stones. Yet money and status could not insulate them from the escalating violence, or from tragedy. My father was one of nine children, but my grandmother gave birth to several more who were stillborn or who died as infants. When war and extremism descended, the local mullahs started speaking against the Ghafari family: one of my father's brothers, Abdul Sami, was a member of the Khalq Party, the same leftist, Soviet-backed bloc that Mohammad Jan from Changa had joined. He believed that the party offered the best ideas for Afghanistan, that it would modernise the country and in particular push for girls to be educated. But according to the mullahs, this made him a non-believer. The family started to leave home less often, preferring to stay behind their gates as everything outside changed beyond recognition. My uncle Abdul Sami was killed in an ambush by the mujahideen, who buried him with one hand sticking out of the ground as a warning. It worked. My father's family left their increasingly hostile village, the place where they had once been so respected. They went to Kabul, fleeing so quickly they had no time to gather any of their precious things. Some of the children were barefoot as they left, my father just eleven years old. They arrived in the capital in the mid-1980s, and while the brothers who were old enough joined the army, the five sisters went out to work.

In the factory they noticed there was something different about my mother, something deeper than her dark-haired beauty. The early loss of her father had instilled in her a quiet resilience, and a tendency to turn her anxieties inwards. She never quite knew how to grieve this man she could not picture, who was nonetheless an essential part of her being. Unable to join in with her mother's reminiscences, instead she filled the blank page with images gathered from a few photographs, creating her own private version of her father in her imagination. It was this man that she mourned, internally. She still does not show her emotions easily.

My father, Abdul Wasi, was intrigued when his sisters talked of this enigmatic girl. He was twenty-seven by then, thirteen years older than my mother, and had followed his brothers into the national army. He drove a Jeep, a symbol of prestige in Kabul. He had once been handsome, with a thick head of glossy black hair and a full moustache. Unfortunately, his most dashing days were behind him. A few years earlier he had been in a battle with the mujahideen in Farah province close to the Iranian border when his Humvee broke down in the middle of Dasht-e Reg Rawan, a deadly desert. The jihadists surrounded the soldiers in their Humvee, exposed in the middle of the empty lunar landscape. They were stuck there, doing everything from eating to going to the toilet inside the vehicle. The temperatures soared to 50 degrees Celsius in the daytime. Every time one of them stuck their head out of the vehicle an unseen mujahid would take a pot shot. It was two weeks before back-up arrived from Kabul, 700 miles away across unforgiving terrain, by which time my father's hair had fallen out. When it grew back it was coarse and a lighter shade of brown.

Some wealthy Afghan families might have looked down on my mother, regarding her as an impoverished girl of few prospects. But to my father's family, it was clear that her circumstances did not reflect her character. Even though she was just a child when my grandfather was murdered, my mother carried some of his dignity in her. She was still going to school despite her family's hardships and the war closing in on Kabul. In fact, it took my father's family six months to persuade my grandmother to allow her daughter to marry their son. Eventually, my paternal grandfather went to the house carrying the holy Quran, and asked my grandmother himself not to say no. My mother and father were married two years later, in 1993, as fighting raged in Kabul.

Against the backdrop of war, my parents' wedding was a rare display of joy and relative opulence, a moment in which the Ghafari family could imagine themselves to be still the rich, respected people they had been back in Herat. It was held in one of the city's two wedding halls, with a filmmaker hired to record it all on VHS.

As children, we used to watch the video with the sound turned down since, by then, the Taliban had banned television. My younger brother Wasil and I would sit on the floor as my dad pulled the set from the back of the cupboard and then plugged in all the cables. In the dark with the curtains closed, the flicker from the screen would illuminate our faces. We were enthralled by the exoticism of it: my mother's heavy make-up, the live music and wedding singer, and when it got to the end we would beg for him to rewind it so we could watch again. As the Taliban dragged Afghanistan back to the Middle Ages, the scenes from the video seemed to have come from the future, not the past.

My mother was sixteen when she married my dad, and

carried on going to school. He took her to the gate every day on the back of his bicycle, until I was born a year later. My father always called me *Sartajak*, the name of a small grey bird you can see swooping over the rooftops of Kabul. He always told me that he prayed that his first child would be a girl, and that I was the answer to his prayer. I am not sure I can explain to you how unusual it is to have an Afghan father use a term of endearment like this, and speak with such affection to his daughter.

I may have inherited my mother's profile, but when I turn to face you straight on you will see nothing but my father. My mother and grandmother have the same broad face, but mine is narrow and angular. In a childhood photo in which I am cuddling into the crook of my father's shoulder, taken when I was six or seven years old, you can already see that the contours of our cheekbones are the same. I also inherited his temperament: there is nothing of my mother's stoic silence in me. I speak the truth I see before me in an instant. My temper is explosive but short-lived, erupting in small bursts throughout the day. If I were to keep it all inside me I would eventually explode like a malfunctioning pressure cooker.

Before I was conceived, and before he had even met my mother, my father had bought me my first toy: an orange teddy bear he brought back from the Soviet Union. He had been sent on a training mission there in the late 1980s, in the final years before Moscow withdrew its army from Afghanistan. By the time he gave it to me, soon after I was born, the army he served was no longer under the Soviet thumb.

Without its patrons, the communist government was

crumbling, and the mujahideen smelled blood. They converged around the capital, Masood and Dostum's forces from the north, and Hekmatyar's from the south. It was Masood's men, numbering some 10,000, who entered Kabul first, in April 1992, helped by mutinous government troops. President Najibullah Ahmadzai, nicknamed 'The Ox' for his demeanour of brutish thuggery, fled, and Masood assembled a coalition government made up of the various mujahideen factions and members of the former regime. The army also pledged its loyalty to Masood.

Within days, battles between the factions had broken out on the streets of Kabul. Hekmatyar stationed his forces on the mountains of Char Asiab, which loom over the southern parts, and fired an endless stream of rockets onto the districts laid out below them. That earned the warlord the nickname Rocketyar – 'friend of the rockets'. In the north, Dostum, the Uzbek leader, was employing the same tactic, positioning his artillery on the mountains there. In the spring of 1994, while my mother was pregnant with me, Hekmatyar added starvation to the list of miseries that Kabul was suffering. He refused to allow UN food convoys to pass through the gate to the city that he controlled, this in addition to the lack of electricity or running water, and hospitals and schools bombed out of use.

The upper-class residential districts in the north and west of Kabul, already largely emptied of their residents, many of whom had fled to Europe and America, were left in ruins by the fighting between the mujahideen. The Darul Aman palace in the south of the city was shelled until its silhouette looked like a set of broken dentures. My parents survived almost entirely on vegetables in that period, my mother taking priority over my father when the meagre meals were served so that I could be nourished in her belly. In September 1994 my mother gave birth to me at home, with the sound of gunfire and mortar strikes echoing in the distance. There were no midwives to help, only her female relatives and in-laws. It might sound like an inauspicious start, but I consider myself lucky. I was born into one of my country's very bleakest periods, yet both my mother and I survived.

Although Masood was considered the most tolerant of all the mujahideen leaders, his men were largely illiterate and strict in their interpretations of Islam. The presenter on the evening television news show, who had once appeared with her hair uncovered, now draped a scarf over her head. On the streets, the miniskirt-wearing students were long gone; almost every woman now wore the *chador*, a loose one-piece cloak covering everything from the top of the head to the floor. There had once been a street in the old city packed with shops that sold second-hand clothes from Western stores, but these closed down as the demand for blue jeans and high heels plummeted – what was the point when there was nowhere to show them off? Outside Kabul, the situation was even worse. In the south of Afghanistan, around the city of Kandahar, one particular mujahideen group was seizing control of a growing area: the Taliban.

These fighters, 'the students', were the protégés of Mullah Omar, a mujahideen commander who had scored few successes on the battlefield in Afghanistan, but real-ised that the generation of young Afghans who were now growing up in refugee camps in Pakistan would make ideal recruits to his cause. In Pakistan's madrassas, or religious seminaries, which gave them a free education (and with such charity these were often a family's only option), the students were schooled in an extreme, unbending version of Islam, which glorified violence and death in the name of jihad. Their lives and families had been fractured, and they were full of fury at the godless invaders who had forced them from their homeland. Mullah Omar convinced them that the other mujahideen groups were no better than the Soviet soldiers, presiding as they were over drug-trafficking and corruption. In the early 1990s, as Masood, Hekmatyar and Dostum entered a power struggle in the main city, the Taliban was advancing through the rest of the country.

The civil war between Masood and the other mujahideen groups raged in the city for four years until, in September 1996, days before my second birthday, Mullah Omar's Talibs entered Kabul. They captured the former president Najibullah Ahmadzai from a UN compound, where he had been preparing to flee to India, murdered him and hung his castrated body alongside his brother's from traffic lights in the central Aryana Square, just outside the presidential palace he had once ruled from. There they remained for two days, a warning to anyone who might try to resist the new order. Few did. The Taliban declared Afghanistan an Islamic emirate, to be governed by a harsh interpretation of Sharia law. The mujahideen warlords and their men had been doing as they pleased when they controlled the city, kidnapping girls to force into marriage, looting homes and businesses and killing their opponents without fear of reprisal. The Taliban promised to put an end to the lawlessness: their strict Sharia rules meant that thieves had their hands cut off and adulterers lost their lives. One teenage boy accused of stealing scrap metal was paraded through the streets in a version of the stocks, his face blackened with soot. The defeated mujahideen, led by Masood, retreated to Panjshir, his mountainous Tajik stronghold north of Kabul.

In the three months after the Taliban took control of Kabul, 50,000 more people fled the city. We stayed because we had no better options. In Kabul, at least, we had a home, whereas elsewhere we would have been dependent on relatives or charity. Government employees like my father were required to carry on signing into work every day, even though there was no longer any work for them to do. At least he still received a salary. Life under the Taliban was less physically dangerous than it had been during the civil war, but it quickly faded to a bleak monochrome thanks to the reams of petty rules that they issued. Birds were banned as pets, and so their cages were opened and scores of canaries and mynah birds fluttered into the wild. Bred in captivity, they were unable to fend for themselves as the winter drew in, and the streets were soon littered with bright yellow carcasses. Card games and chess, believed to encourage gambling, were outlawed, along with football, which was deemed un-Islamic. Kite-flying, a popular hobby, was banned and so too were paper bags, lest a page of the Quran end up being repurposed as one. For women, the rules were even stricter. My mother could no longer leave the house unless she was covered from head to toe in a burka with just a small embroidered grille to peer through, and even then, only if she was accompanied by my father or one of her brothers. Television, dancing and all music apart from Islamic incantations were banned. My father stashed our television set away, and the unspooled tape of cassettes that the Taliban had seized fluttered from Kabul's lamp posts, something that, in my childlike way, I considered a jolly sight. Men were forced to grow out their beards and to attend mosque five times a day. The vice and virtue police meted out punishments – whipping, stoning and maiming – to anyone found non-compliant. Adultery, drinking alcohol and murder were punishable by death.

Life for ordinary Afghan men under the new regime was reduced to work, home and the mosque. For most women, work and mosque were taken out of the equation. For girls, there was no school, let alone university – the 4,000 women who had been studying at Kabul University were ordered home. Women were allowed to work, but only if they had jobs in health care, since male doctors were banned from treating women. Girls were expected to wear the burka from the time they turned ten years old.

My parents shielded us from politics. I remember all of us staying with relatives in a neighbourhood called Makroyan, a geometric maze of Soviet-built apartment blocks in east Kabul, where residents strung out their washing between their windows and lines of gangly trees. The neighbourhood's once-verdant public spaces were now littered with informal cemeteries filled with the bodies of residents killed during the civil war. The graves were hastily marked, sometimes just a few stones laid on top marking out the resting place of a loved relative. Within a few months of the Taliban taking power, hyperinflation had taken hold in the food markets. Kabul's poverty was so bad that children were digging up human bones to sell to traders, who exported them to Pakistan where they were ground up and added to chickenfeed. Yet when the blocks were constructed in the late 1960s they had been cutting-edge, with central heating systems. And though they were grubby and run-down by the time we lived there, and those public spaces filled with death, Makroyan remained one of the better neighbourhoods. The Soviet design, although ugly, was sturdy, and the blocks had withstood the rocket attacks better than most other buildings. Lined up row after row like soldiers, they made us feel protected.

Later we moved in with two of my uncles and my maternal grandmother, whom we called Bobo Jan. She was a stout, quiet-voiced woman whose calm demeanour was at odds with her inner strength. In this household she was the matriarch, her top-floor front room the venue for all our family gatherings. The house was in Kart-e Naw, a sprawling place in the south of the city which had been nothing but villages and pasture until developers arrived in the 1950s. By the time we were living there it was a land of narrow alleys and concrete, but still most houses had no running water. There were communal wells or, for the slightly better-off, fountains in the yards of the buildings. Otherwise, water was bought from vendors who manoeuvred their carts laden with huge metal flagons down the alleyways, and who would herald their arrival with a drawn-out note of rising intonation. The area had once been one of the city's most multicultural, with Pashtun, Dari, Tajik and Uzbek living together. But when it fell under the control of the mujahideen forces during the civil war, many of its original residents fled. By the time the Taliban arrived, people were trickling back to Kart-e Naw, but now they were mostly Pashtun – that rich tapestry could not be re-stitched so easily. Later, in another neighbourhood, we lived in an apartment on the fifth floor and I would sit at the window, looking out for my friend Tamara passing below. When I saw her, I would race out and we would go to the playground to meet my cousins. At the neighbourhood wedding parties the women would deck themselves out in jewellery and illegal nail polish, and sing in low voices so that any passing Taliban patrol would not hear. With music banned, the women would tap on small drums called *darya*.

My father continued working under every new regime, and so he continued under the Taliban. He was promoted to the rank of colonel the same year they took Kabul, but by then the Afghan national army had been reduced to little more than a vassal of the mujahideen groups. Under the Taliban it limped on, though it was the jihadist fighters and the mullahs who now held the real power. Still, my father's position meant he could push his luck a bit further than most. Occasionally, as a change from the wedding video, my father ran a thin wire from our secret television's aerial socket onto the balcony and up to the washing line. With that, we could pick up a fuzzy Iranian signal. Even the most mundane programme from the Islamic theocracy next door seemed daring and glamorous to us. We would sit in front of the muted television, transfixed by the keep-fit programmes that were all the rage in the mid-nineties. They were presented by headscarved women in baggy clothes, entirely unsuitable for the energetic step exercises they were demonstrating.

For the grown-ups, the Taliban made useful bogey-men. Their appearance – locks of long hair protruding from huge turbans, kohl-lined eyes glaring out from sun-hammered faces – was striking enough to spark all kinds of childish nightmares. As I walked through the streets with my grandma Bobo Jan, laughing and shouting as she tried to hurry me along, she would beseech me to stop being so naughty: 'If you don't behave properly,' she told me, 'the Taliban will come and get you.'

I did not realise when I started school, aged four, that I was engaging in an act of resistance. If my parents had been caught, they would have been arrested and tortured. My teacher would most likely have been executed. But for me it was entirely normal that, each morning, I would leave our apartment, skip around the corner to a nearby apartment, almost identical to ours, and there descend to the basement. I sat together with the other girls, cross-legged on a rug, and each morning went through the same ritual. The teacher would say good morning to us and then we would greet the teacher and each other in a sing-song, rhythmic reply. We learnt the rudiments of the Dari language, a tongue close to Farsi that is the lingua franca in diverse Kabul, and English from the yellowed pages of two well-worn textbooks. I remember the struggle of writing from left to right for the first time – both Dari and Pashto are written from right to left – and how plain the English letters seemed next to the baroque curls of the Arabic alphabet. My first English words were simple syllables that I would repeat over and over, curling my lips as I tried to get the vowel sounds right: *Book. Pen. Truck. Ball.* There were small, badly placed windows at the top of the room, and we never put the lights on, so we studied in the murky darkness. If there were footsteps outside our teacher would shush us and gesture for us to hide our books under the carpet. Sometimes we had to hold our breath until the sound of footsteps had retreated. When we sang the national anthem each morning, she implored us to keep our voices low. That was something I never understood: the words were all about how wonderful Afghanistan was, and I believed it! So why weren't we allowed to shout it out at the top of our lungs? It was only years later that I realised it was the Taliban she was afraid of.

For the most part, my primary school days were filled with the same childhood games and friendships as yours. Each day, after our lessons ended, I would walk part of the way home with classmates. When it came to the point where we separated, them going to their street and me going to mine, we would repeat the same nonsensical question-and-answer nursery rhymes to each other.

'I have one rupee, what should we buy?' one of us would shout.

And then another would reply: 'Let's buy this one! And now – time to go home!' And that would be the signal to run as fast as possible, all the way back to our homes.

But I was also aware right from the start that, somehow, I did not fit in. I was never the most popular in my class, neither during those Taliban times nor in later years. I was years younger than most of the other girls in my basement school and they took full advantage of my naivety. One day, as I was walking to class, I caught up with three girls who were carrying teapots and glasses in thin arms stretching out from under their burkas.

'It's Teachers' Day!' they cried when they saw me, empty-handed. 'You won't be allowed into class if you don't bring anything for the picnic!'

I believed them, of course, and ran home to tell my mother. She quickly gathered some sweets into a bag for me and boiled up a pot of fresh tea. By the time I reached class, half-running while trying not to spill the scalding liquid on myself, I was late and the girls were laughing at me. But I did not care – I wanted to impress the teacher. She was the most stylish lady I had ever seen, with the palest skin and bright red lipstick. She had lived in the United States for some years but decided to come back to Afghanistan to help girls like me.

My mother, herself an educated woman, could now only live vicariously through me. By the time I started school, women had disappeared under a thousand Taliban rules. Our windows, like everyone else's, had to be painted over to prevent anyone looking in from outside. On the rare occasions my mother did go out onto the streets she had to walk without making a sound. Each day when I got home from school she would greet me at the door, ask me what I had learned, and sit down to help me with my homework. I sang the poems my mother taught me, and together we would repeat English words and phrases again and again, until they cemented themselves into my brain.

The last time I went down into one of those Kabul basements it was night time. It was early October 2001 and the air already had a chilly grip. My parents shook us awake. We were four by that time: I was seven; my brothers, Wasil, four years old and Wasel eighteen months; and tiny, red-faced Horya, had been born three months earlier. My mother said we had to go to the neighbour's house, and we shuffled down there with tired eyes and some blankets and oil lamps. The bombing started soon after, the impacts rolling like a steam train through the ground towards us; my parents had heard on the radio that the US President George W. Bush had ordered attacks on Afghanistan to start. I was sure the building might collapse on top of us, and huddled deeper under my blanket. I had never really known anything of war before that night, even though my country had been defined by it for decades. In fact, those first American bombs of 2001 fell on Bibi Mahru hill, right behind our house in Makroyan. It was once a popular spot for walking and picnicking, with impressive panoramic views over the city, but the Taliban had a radar base there and the people who lived around it had already abandoned their homes, sure that their area would be first when the strikes came. For me and my siblings, it came out of nowhere – our parents had told us nothing about the September 11 attacks, nor the growing focus on Afghanistan in the capitals of the West. Just as they had shielded us from the politics of our country, they shielded us from the fact that we were now at the epicentre of an earthquake shaking the world.

They could not close our eyes to what was happening on the streets outside. The next morning, hours after the last bomb had fallen, my parents sent me out to get bread from a local bakery. I saw the corpse from a hundred metres away, looking like a pile of rags dumped by the side of the street at the bottom of Bibi Mahru hill. As I got closer I saw that a hand and a foot had been dismembered in the blast

34

that killed him, and that they were lying some distance away. The hand was unnaturally white, I remember, and the blood that had drained out of it was smeared on the road. Everyone else was just walking past, and so I did the same. The body belonged to a Taliban fighter, and nobody was sure what the protocol was for burying them. I had only seen a dead body once before, that of my paternal grandfather, a huge man laid out neatly in his coffin. This body was different; its brokenness sickened me. I stopped and stood there for what felt like a very long time, trying to work out how a person could be twisted into such angles. I thought about that orange teddy that my father had bought for me. It was as though I had taken that teddy and pulled at it until its fabric tore and the stuffing spilled out. And the colours were so unnatural too: the blood was not the bright red that trickled from cuts in my knees when I stumbled in the street. This blood had turned to dark brown in the hours since it had left the fighter's body. The other thing that was strange was how the adults were just hurrying past it, as though it were just another piece of litter on the street. I could not make it to the bakery, and returned home empty-handed and nauseated.

The US reported that it had launched 'surgical strikes' on that first night of the war, taking out the Taliban's critical infrastructure while avoiding civilian deaths. The people of Bibi Mahru returned to their homes, but ten days later American jets flew back to strike the village again. This time, their bombs hit homes, not a Taliban position several hundred metres away. Ten people were killed, and soon similar strikes were happening all over Kabul, and then all over the country.

Soon, the country filled with pink-faced, blond, giant-like soldiers who kicked in the doors of family homes and dragged men and boys off to prison. The bombings never got any more surgical: 71,000 civilians were killed in Afghanistan and Pakistan over the twenty years of America's war; four in ten of those deaths were the result of airstrikes. For each one of those dead, there was an extended family left traumatised, angry and often thirsty for vengeance. Who offered the chance to strike back at the foreign invaders? The Taliban, taking on the very same role the mujahideen had twenty-five years before. And so, Afghanistan's cycle of invasion and extremism started again.

Kabul, once the safest part of Afghanistan, fell in America's cross hairs. As the bombings continued, night after night, the Northern Alliance, a coalition of mujahideen groups and US special forces, inched their way towards the capital. My parents decided it was not safe for us to stay, and so we gathered our documents and most important household possessions, then crammed into a car and drove away. It was my first time leaving Kabul; until then, my world hadn't extended much beyond the edges of my neighbour-hood. Driving west out of the city, the road gradually grew more pockmarked until eventually it became just a track. For hours we bumped along it in boneshaking fashion. I remember how the smell of the air changed, how the pollution and sewage smells lifted as we left the last Kabul neighbourhoods behind. On the mountain roads, we were enveloped by an alien quiet and the sweet floral scent of the *sinjid* tree, whose tiny yellow flowers turn into delicious rusty red nuts. It felt like we had entered a different universe, but in fact, we had driven just twenty-five miles, to my father's home province of Wardak. For millennia Wardak has been a frontier, the gateway to Kabul that invaders all covet. Wardak's terrain is difficult to conquer, riddled with precipitous mountains and gushing rivers. Perhaps that is why it is filled with some of Afghanistan's most stubborn, rebellious people – the Pashtun tribes who put up a fierce resistance against the British during their attempt to conquer Afghanistan in the nineteenth century, and who a century later formed the core of the Taliban.

My father's family village, Dawran Khel, sits on the Chak river, which cuts an emerald-green slice through the mountains. In Kabul it was the street sellers and the mosque's call to prayer that woke me each morning, but here it was birdsong and the gurgling of the stream that ran close to my great-uncle's house, where we stayed with my father's sister and brother. It was a sprawling place, so different to our tight apartment blocks, though all six of us – my parents, my three siblings and I – had just one room to stay in. Cows wandered outside. There was so much less to be scared of here, yet it was a much more conservative society than I was used to. The women wore long dresses and were swathed in scarves, even though there were no Taliban checkpoints and patrols to worry about. Even stranger for me was that everyone spoke Pashto; though it is the language of my ethnic group, I barely knew it – I had grown up speaking Dari, as had my mother. My cousin Qabila and I had to work out a common way of communicating, but once we did we became inseparable. The month spent in the village passed in *Swallows and*

Amazons-type adventures for me. We would often picnic, taking huge pieces of bread, corn and potatoes all wrapped in fabric, and set out across the tiny roads and fields. Qabila would build an oven out of stone, we'd light a fire inside it, and then put another stone on top. Like that we'd cook the corn until it turned into popcorn, and heat the bread and any other vegetables we had with us. We would go to the orchards that belonged to our family and pick cherries, quince and apricots. The flavours of the food we cooked there were more intense, more earthy than anything I had tasted in Kabul. The women would milk the cows to make thick-skinned yoghurt which my mother would gulp down from its clay pot. There was a huge tandoor oven in the front yard, which they kept hot almost all the time. In the evening, when it was fully fired up, we would put the meat and vegetables in it for our supper, and then use the remaining heat to cook flatbreads that my aunties slapped onto the side of the tandoor. I was always in awe of how they did it with their bare arms, with such skill that they never burned themselves.

Qabila, who was only a few years older than me, was by then already wearing the same outfit as the middle-aged women – a billowing cloak over her clothes and a long headscarf covering every strand of her hair. She had never been to school, and is now a housewife, still living in the same village with three children of her own – a wonderful woman, but illiterate, cut off from the opportunities that even the most basic level of education would have afforded her.

In Kabul, the war ended quickly; the Taliban simply melted away. It was never a natural home for the village boys: the urbanites of Kabul had always loathed them. In Wardak, my parents followed the news on the radio. It filtered down to me, aged seven, through snippets of the adults' conversations; although I didn't understand the politics, I knew that something huge was happening in my country. I pieced together the broad contours of events from the words that cropped up most often: *bombs, America, Taliban, defeat.* I learned about the September 11 attacks for the first time on the national television channel, Milli TV, and from there began piecing together the reasons why our lives had been so abruptly interrupted. I also started to realise that Kabul would not be the same when we returned. Television programming had begun airing at 6 p.m. with the national anthem: 'Fortress of Islam, Heart of Asia'. Even with its overtly Islamist lyrics, we had never heard it under the Taliban – it, like all other music with instruments, was banned.

We returned to Kabul in mid-November; it had taken just a month for the US and the Northern Alliance to drive the Taliban out. In fact, the Taliban regime was collapsing in cities all over the country. In the space of five days, six provincial capitals fell. The Talibs who survived fled to the countryside, where they disappeared into the mountains and villages. The Americans now trained their sights on the Tora Bora mountains, to the east of Kabul near the Pakistan border, where they believed Osama bin Laden to be hiding out. Meanwhile, Afghans like us were left to begin adjusting to another new regime.

The first time I saw my mother leave the house in Kabul without her blue burka I was stunned. It took her a while to build up the confidence to do it – after years under a shroud, throwing it off is not so easy. Other women took smaller steps; they continued to wear the burka but flaunted a flash of bare ankle. Our TV was now a source of news, as well as entertainment; from the news reports on Milli TV we learned that Hamid Karzai, a Pashtun leader who had been living in exile in Pakistan, had returned to Afghanistan and been appointed head of the transitional government, and then later that he had won the presidential election. Out on the streets, the mood was tangibly lighter without the scowling, long-haired Taliban fighters milling around. Businesses started up, taking advantage of all the new freedoms and all the extra requirements those freedoms entailed. Colour televisions became a status symbol, but since the electricity was patchy generators were needed to run them. The most popular generator was the Tiger, dinky, blue and black, and Chinese-made. It ran on gasoline, and soon the fumes of a million Tigers added to Kabul's soupy polluted evening air. Markets selling bootleg music and films mushroomed around Kabul. We got our first colour TV set, along with a CD player and a generator, in 2002, when I was eight. To christen it, my father rented a Bollywood film called *The Heart Is Crazy*, the story of a tangle of love affairs between the members of a dance troupe. The screening was an extended family gathering, my grandmother and uncles packing into our front room with us to witness this exciting new milestone in our improved lives. The dialogue was in Hindi and there were no subtitles, so none of us could understand a word. It didn't matter. Watching the uncovered women with their elegant, figure-hugging clothes, and the handsome men they flirted with so openly, was like witnessing alien life. I remember one scene with a woman in a black miniskirt and white shirt dancing in the open as people sat watching and eating ice cream. We sat in silence for the whole three hours, utterly transfixed by this world we had been cut off from for so long.

We didn't realise it at the time but we were living through Kabul's golden era. From the fall of the Taliban until 2008, the city was safe and booming. Tourists started visiting Afghanistan – unthinkable before – and it was safe for women to walk the streets alone. Shops and restaurants were opening, and with them a kind of social life I had never seen. The flood of foreign soldiers and aid workers brought with it a flotsam of international restaurants – Thai, sushi and pizza became fashionable among young Kabul elites although, secretly, most of us still preferred *bolani*, a vegetable-filled flatbread served fresh and hot by vendors at the roadside. A café culture of sorts sprang up in the backstreets: clean, cosy spaces hosting mixed groups of men and women, almost unheard of previously. There was also a sudden boom in wedding halls; the best of them modelled on the Taj Mahal, with golden domes and huge stained-glass windows. Most Afghan weddings used to happen at home, with men and women strictly separated, but it became the urban fashion for couples to parade through the city in a hooting convoy and then sit on thrones in front of hundreds of guests. There was a rush for wedding singers, who often had to squeeze several gigs into one night, such was the demand. The building boom stretched to the residential sector, too: the nouveau riche favoured a baroque style of mansion, built in a confused mix of classicism and Gaudi-esque surreal. For the more modest Kabuli there were the newer apartment blocks – nothing much to look at but palaces compared to the places we grew up in.

The main difference for me was that I was now, aged seven, going to school openly for the first time in my life. Karzai made education a priority in the post-Taliban Afghanistan, particularly for girls, who had been mostly deprived for nearly a decade. Naswan-e Rahman Mina school was the first girls' school to open in our area, and it was just a short distance from our house in Kart-e Naw. Every day I walked there proudly in my uniform, a black dress with white headscarf, past the old Aryoub cinema, once one of the most fashionable destinations in the city. It had been abandoned in the Taliban era and was dilapidated. Sometimes, when I had a spare ten minutes, I would go in there and roam around, drunk on the freedom of exploring a hidden world in the heart of the city. When I started at the Naswan-e Rahman Mina the classrooms had not even been prepared and we took our first lessons in tents erected in the yard. The building was nothing special, particularly compared to the boys' school, which was a palatial modern complex. But when I first stepped inside I was overwhelmed with excitement – there were desks, and blackboards! Before starting I had to take an aptitude test, which placed me in the fourth grade. Aged seven, I was the youngest in my class since most of the other girls had never been to school. I had to stand up behind my desk because I was too short to see the blackboard over the heads of the other girls when I sat down. I was too young and shy to battle with the other girls for a better spot, though later my teachers moved my place to the front of the class. At that time history was my favourite subject. I became obsessed with the news and political discussion programmes, listening intently as my parents' guests argued over the big issues of the day. Later, one of the girls in my class brought a frog into school for us to dissect in our biology lesson, and from then on science became my passion. I never forgot about history and geography, but now I also loved becoming absorbed in the minutiae of a mathematics problem, homing in on the smallest detail which held the key to a whole equation.

Every day, at break time, the teachers handed out packets of Indian-made biscuits and after school we would visit the street vendors to buy ice cream and grape juice. Sometimes the American soldiers would come into our school, looking like characters from an action movie in their sunglasses and armour. They were huge, and somewhat scary, but kind: they would hand out pens and sweets to us, and I was always chosen to speak with them since I spoke English better than the other girls – not great by any means, but I knew some words and was confident enough to use them. I felt that my life was opening up, that from here on my freedoms would only increase. I started to have ambitions, dreams of what I could be. I didn't feel there were any limits on me. One of my father's sisters was married to a man who had been Afghanistan's ambassador in the US.

I could do that, I thought.

I decided I should study political science at university, mapping out my life path already even though I was still a tiny girl. Every day, I felt happy as I walked to my school.

*

At home, the mood was less celebratory. In late 2002, my father lost his job. The military was one of Karzai's first targets as he set about rebuilding the country, and it was completely disarmed and disbanded and then built up again from scratch. My father, who had worked as a trainer at one of the military colleges, tried to find work as a day-labourer in Sar-e Chawk, a huge roundabout in the centre of Kabul which had turned into a kind of makeshift Job Centre. He would come home with his hands bleeding, the result of hauling masonry, until eventually my mother and I pleaded with him not to do that work any more. He started speaking with his old military friends, asking around for jobs that might be opening in the new Afghan national army.

One day, in 2003, he struck lucky: there was a posting for him in Paktia, a rough tribal area in the east of Afghanistan – the home of the Tora Bora mountains. Taking the job meant he would be away for months at a time. Yet it was not something he could turn down. For more than a year, my father served long, lonely postings in Paktia, taking days to snap out of his dark mood when he returned home for breaks. The road was growing dangerous as the Taliban began to regroup, outweighing the danger of moving his whole family to the east. So in 2004, my father decided that we should join him in Paktia.

Two

Afghanistan is a harsh country. War and dictatorship have that effect on a nation and its people. My father saw the worst of it: the bloodthirsty mujahideen and the dangers awaiting women who ventured out on the streets. He was enrolled at the military high school when he was nine, moulded along the lines of rank, protocol and discipline. He ran our household like an army unit – he was the commander and we were the soldiers under his charge. His tall stature was amplified by his rigid, upright posture, and even when I was an adult, it always seemed to me that he was a giant. Under the Taliban he had been forced to grow out his beard, and the ring of coarse fuzz softened the sharp angles of his face. But he was one of those who, as soon as that regime was toppled, headed straight to the barber for a clean shave. Five years of being dictated to on the streets had not changed his soldierly demeanour. Everything had to be clean and tidy when he came home in the evenings; if a jumper or a bag or anything else were left scattered he would notice straight away and demand that it be corrected immediately. Sometimes he couldn't bear to wait for someone else to sort it out, and would start tidying up himself, even before he had changed out of his uniform. I have inherited his obsessive-compulsive tendencies: when I see a book sticking out of the shelf or a stray hair on the floor, I cannot relax until it is dealt with. If I see a smear on a mirror I will clean it with my headscarf.

Our relationship was like Tom and Jerry, two stubborn-headed personalities, allies and enemies by turn. We loved to have long, light-hearted arguments, debating everything from the best Afghan dish to the merits of various politicians. But I could only spar with him like that when he was in a good mood. When he was brooding I couldn't speak to him. He had the kind of expressive face that made it easy to tell what he was feeling: if he was upset, his dark eyebrows knitted and his eyes seemed to focus on something that wasn't there.

His high standards meant I never thought of myself as a girl; after all, I had as many responsibilities as an eldest son. In the winter, if my parents were busy it was I who headed up onto the roof to clear off the snow with a shovel taller than I was, even when my younger brothers were big enough to help out. When my siblings were play-fighting and pouring water all over the house, I was the one who shouldered the punishment, even though I had tried my best to stop them. As I got older my father became stricter, expecting more from me while allowing less. If I could not solve a mathematics problem, or if I had ripped a page out of my school exercise book, he would demand to know why, and then thread a pen between my fingers and twist it until I cried out in pain. Increasingly, I was kept inside the house with the other women, banned from playing with the other children on my street. As I grew up, it seemed he was endowing me with a mind, while snatching away my chance to use it.

The move to Paktia at the age of nine felt like a step back. It seemed to me a scary, lawless place. Pakistan's tribal areas, home to the refugee camps and religious schools where the Taliban was formed, start just a few miles east of Gardez, the district capital. It was a shame the area had become so tarnished by violence and militancy, because its geography rivals that of the Alps. Of the 234 named mountains packed into this comparatively small province, Sikaram Sar is the tallest, soaring nearly 5,000 metres into the heavens. In spring they are blanketed by a vivid green canvas, and studded with wildflowers and pine forests; in winter they are capped with snow so crisp that the sunlight bounces off, as if refracted by diamonds. But the soft sandstone of the border mountains is riddled with cave and tunnel networks which were dug by the mujahideen during the Soviet war, and then taken over by smugglers during Taliban times. In 2001, this was where many Taliban fighters went to ground, and then escaped over the border into Pakistan where they would soon regroup and start planning their revenge, with the support of the Pakistani intelligence services, the Inter-Services Intelligence, or ISI. Bin Laden was believed to have been whisked away to Paktia's Tora Bora mountain range in 2001. Later he too fled to Pakistan, where he lived comfortably in a compound close to Abbottabad, until he was killed by US Navy Seals in May 2011.

The insurgency in Paktia was almost a war in itself, conducted by a discrete unit of the Taliban with even stronger ties to Pakistan than to the rest of the group. The region had long held a kind of semi-autonomy, with its Pashtun tribes once exempt from paying taxes thanks to their century-long loyalty to the Afghan kings, and then to the central government. In fact, the Pashtun of Paktia are suspicious of those of Kandahar, where the Taliban has its origins. But at the same time, the area was racked by the inter-mujahideen fighting of the early 1990s, and so in 1995 its tribal leaders welcomed the Taliban when the group swept in.

In 2001 it was the local Paktia Pashtun tribes who overthrew the Taliban, kicking them out of the province in November, a day after the Northern Alliance entered Kabul. But almost immediately the US made a grave error. Four days after the province had fallen, American bombers launched strikes on the town of Gardez. Bombs fell on homes and shops, killing scores of civilians. Worse, the US kept repeating their mistake, partly because of their lack of contacts and sources on the ground. On one occasion, the Americans bombed a convoy carrying a tribal delegation to the inauguration of Hamid Karzai in Kabul. Meanwhile, Paktia's tribal elders felt they were being excluded from the power deals being cut in Kabul, and that the Tajik-dominated Northern Alliance was receiving a disproportionate amount of US backing. Later, they also complained of being excluded from Karzai's cabinet. And in this fertile environment, insurgency took root, dug in deep amid those fearsome, beautiful mountains.

Bin Laden had probably already fled Paktia by the time

we arrived there, in 2004. But there were still thousands, maybe tens of thousands, of his sympathisers in this province, and they were determined to wind back any liberalising changes that had been ushered into Afghan society with the fall of the Taliban. They were also determined to spill the blood of the infidel invaders. The US soldiers stationed here did not bring pens into primary schools and smile at us, as they had in Kabul. The intelligence networks America had managed to build in other parts of the country hit a dead end in Paktia, and the soldiers knew they were stepping deep into enemy territory. They watched their backs, all day every day, twitchy and aggressive with fear.

Although we had always been poor, we lived in places that were at least well-maintained and surrounded by big city amenities. My father had used a beautifully deep red paint on some of the walls of our flat in Kabul, and done the rest a contrasting off-white, and our living space was comfortable and filled with light. Our new house in Gardez was completely different – in a far smaller building than the huge apartment blocks I was used to. Another family lived in a building across our shared yard. Their mother, a widow, had many children ranging from young teenagers to men in their early twenties. The woman earned money by sewing blankets and cushions, and her sons by working as mechanics at a workshop down the road. Both our house and hers were grim, with low ceilings and hardly any natural light. There was no specific room to be used as a kitchen, and the toilet was outside. It was the first time I had ever used a squat toilet – just a hole in the floor, with no running water. The smell was horrendous; whenever I went in there I would wrap my scarf around my nose and try not to breathe. I was always scared of falling down that hole.

Our building was attached at its rear to a small parade of shops, and my mother was terrified that someone might climb over the roofs and come into our house. Though we were living in the centre of the regional capital, to us it felt like a village, all single-storey buildings and streets that went pitch black after the sun went down. Unpaved roads meant dust and mud got everywhere, coating the rugs and leaving a fine brown film on the windows only hours after we'd washed them.

When my father was out on a night shift the rest of us would sleep in the same room, huddling together for warmth and security. The first time it rained, the roof leaked. At first we put buckets and bowls wherever the water dripped down, then later my father bought huge tarpaulins and fixed them to the ceilings and walls. The snow on the roof collected in undulating piles, melting in the places where the heat from our stove escaped. Even when I was wearing the thick gloves that my mother had knitted for me the cold of the shovel's metal handle would seep through to my hands, and by the time I came inside my fingers were bright red and painful.

In the daytimes, we led similar lives as we had in Kabul. My mother had been a teacher after the fall of the Taliban, and soon she started working at a primary school. When she came home from her first day working in Paktia she could not stop talking about the poverty of the children she was meant to be teaching. My father listened impassively as she described how they were malnourished, unclean, and unable to understand anything she was trying to teach them. He was used to the deprivations of Paktia by now, but I was agape at how other people in my country were living. The previous teacher had been running the class as a babysitting service, killing time with the students until the bell rang at the end of the day. The equipment was broken, and there were no curtains up at the windows. My mother bought some light fabric to cover the bare glass, and asked my father to build a small cupboard, which they hauled into the front of the classroom. She filled it with shampoo, nail clippers, soaps, flannels, combs, needle and thread, and every time one of her students arrived unkempt she would wash their hair, face and hands, and help them mend their clothes. After two or three months they were transformed into excellent students.

I also began school in Paktia, but realised from the start that I stuck out. On my first day the girls stared at me when I got on the bus, then snickered behind their hands at my outfit. They were talking Pashto, like my cousin Qabila in Wardak, but in the couple of years that had passed since that idyllic autumn in the countryside I had forgotten the scraps of the language that I had learnt. I couldn't under-stand what they were saying, but I could guess by their unkind glances. I was wearing the same uniform that I had worn to school in Kabul, with a short coat over my trousers and my white scarf around my neck. It was hardly a daring outfit but to them it was something outrageous and alien.

What are they laughing at? I thought. They were the ones

shrouded in billowing over-dresses that tripped them up as they walked. But soon, I felt the pressure to fit in. It is not easy as a nine-year-old girl to be different, particularly when everyone else is pointing it out. My father bought me one of those dresses that I had scorned on the first day, and a huge baggy coat with a big belt to go over it. I hated it. I wore it on the way to school, and covered my hair with my scarf, an unusual, restrictive feeling at first. But my dress and demeanour were still remarkable enough that my teacher singled me out. He always gave me low marks, without even looking at what I had written.

My younger brother Wasel hated Paktia, too, and cried so hard on his first day at school that my mother took him into her own class for a while. All the children in the city seemed so quiet, so withdrawn and controlled compared to my boisterous friends in Kabul. On the street I would gawp in horror at the little girls, just fifty centimetres tall and battling with headscarves a metre long. A family who lived next door to us had a daughter – Fazila – who was my age and who quickly became my friend; however, I soon realised that her life was different to mine. Fazila didn't go to school, and her imperious little brother would order her about, even though he was younger than us. If she disobeyed him, that little pasha would raise his hand and strike her around the face; a seven-year-old boy acting like a man. One day, when I visited Fazila's house at lunch time, I saw the men tucking into a huge platter of *danda-kai*, a dish of rice mixed with juicy lamb meat. *Dandakai* is delicious; as the smell hit my nose my mouth watered. I wanted some, too, but I saw that the women were not eating; they were huddled in the corner, waiting their turn which would only come once the men had filled their bellies. I had never seen such a thing in Kabul.

After five months at the primary school, my mother took a job with the International Rescue Committee, one of the aid organisations that flooded into Afghanistan after 2001. Her duty was to monitor the training of midwives, part of a massive humanitarian effort to improve maternal and infant health care. There were only a handful of gynaecologists in Paktia, where the sparse population is scattered across a wild mountainous landscape, but after 2001 midwifery boomed as a career choice for educated Afghan women like my mother who were desperate to get back into the workplace. Even the most controlling, conservative husband had few grounds to complain about his wife taking a job that revolved entirely around contact with other women. My father, although he might have seemed authoritarian for the restrictions he put on me, was open-minded by Afghan standards and never complained about my mother working outside the house. He saw how unhappy she was in the Taliban years, how frustrating it was staying within the four walls of our home, and since he truly loved her, he wanted her to be content. For me, growing up with a working mother was both an inspiration and a source of resentment. It was rare among my friends, and I felt proud and sophisticated to have a mother who left home each morning and took on an entirely different role. In Paktia, one of her colleagues, an American lady called Rose, would sometimes visit our house after work. I was in awe of her – she was a beautiful Black lady with an afro hairstyle who always wore red lipstick, and when my sister

Marina was born in November 2004, Rose came to congratulate us, bringing a horse toy as a present for the new baby. Such things gave me a window into a world outside Afghanistan that few of my peers at school had. But at the same time, seeing my mother enjoying such freedom made me wonder why my father was always saying no to me. He never explained that he did it out of love, and fear of what might happen to me on the dangerous streets of Paktia. It was only years later that I realised that he did not want me to associate going to school with terror and blood.

Midwives earned impressive wages by Afghan standards, especially those who were employed by the aid agencies, which paid them in foreign currency. Suddenly, an extra two hundred US dollars a month was coming into our household budget, doubling what my father earned. At around the same time, my dad was given a piece of land by the army. We started to build our own home, which was still under construction the first time I saw it, but gave me a rising thrill to know it belonged fully to us. There was a garage for my father's Jeep and, even more exciting, a bedroom just for me. When the house was finished, it was big enough for me to have my own bedroom. It was the first time I had slept in a room by myself; before, I had always been with my siblings and sometimes with my parents, too. But after the novelty wore off, I was scared! The roof was flimsy, and I could hear mice and scorpions scuttling over it at night.

Still, it was clear that our situation had improved. We were no longer just another poor family in Paktia. When one of my friend's sisters celebrated her birthday, I agonised over what I should give her. Celebrating birthdays with presents and cake was not a normal thing in Afghanistan at that time, but this girl had been born in one of the refugee camps in Pakistan and spent the first years of her life there. She had returned to Afghanistan with habits that seemed foreign to the older generations. It was a mark of how far Afghanistan had deteriorated in just five years of Taliban rule that even the Afghans who had spent that time impoverished in exile seemed sophisticated to us. My mum and dad celebrated our birthdays just by giving us a small gift and taking a photo for our family album, to mark how much we had grown. We never had cake. But I did not want to appear to her as a backward Afghan girl. After all, we had gone up in the world! I decided to take her some eggs. My mother had just boiled twenty of them for our breakfast. In a flourish of benevolence, I swept all twenty into a basket and carried them over to my friend's house. I felt like such a grown-up as I handed them over!

My friend's mother didn't know what to say – inside she must have been in hysterics at the sight of me, though she managed to keep a stern expression on her face.

'I have to ask your mother if this is OK!' she said.

I brushed aside her concerns with my hand, and we shared the eggs out between us. I still laugh whenever I think of my younger self playing the rich local lady with a basket of hard-boiled eggs.

As our family's circumstances improved, the security in Paktia worsened. The Taliban had once been squeamish about killing Afghan civilians, but times had changed and now schools had become a frontline in their insurgency. In March 2006 Mohammed Hanif, the head of the Taliban's leadership council, issued a statement raging against the new education system, claiming that the curriculum was designed to brainwash pupils. He singled out the girls' schools in particular, saying that it was 'not acceptable to any Afghan' that girls could be educated without wearing the headscarf, nor for American soldiers to visit their classes. Across the country more than three hundred schools were torched, or closed down before the arsonists could get to them. Teachers and students were attacked as they walked to and from school. By 2006, 100,000 Afghan children who had started school in 2003 and 2004 had dropped out. The main perpetrators of the attacks were the Taliban, of course, but Hekmetyar's men were also thought to be behind some of them. They saw the burgeoning education sector as one of the most visible signs of Afghanistan's new colonisers: the Western diplomats and aid workers. They didn't want Afghan children to be educated anywhere other than the religious seminaries, and, in the case of girls, they didn't want them to be educated at all. Moreover, the schools made an easy target – they didn't tend to be surrounded by razor wire and armed guards, unlike most government and military buildings.

Though Paktia was the first province to receive reconstruction funds for education, it was also one of the first to slip back under the control of the religious fanatics. In October 2005 gunmen stormed a mosque in the Zurmat district, and killed two men including a school caretaker. Seven months later, in the same district, an anti-tank mine was detonated close to a school. In 2007, attackers killed a teacher who was running English language courses. Teachers regularly received death threats, stamped with the seal of armed groups and pinned to their front doors in the dead of night. Most schools, particularly those in rural areas and teaching girls, had been shuttered. By 2006 there was only one school in the whole province – mine – that was still educating girls beyond eighth grade.

Even the president had problems coming to Paktia. At the start of the school year in 2004 we found out that Hamid Karzai was going to visit our schools in Gardez, in a show of support for equal education for boys and girls. I was chosen to be part of a group that would welcome him as his helicopter landed on the playing fields of the boys' school. We were going to sing songs for him, and I hoped I would be allowed to ask him at least one question. It seemed as if we waited for hours, standing under the burning hot sun. I was hungry and my legs were aching, but I knew it would be worth it when the moment came. I was going to meet the president! Even as a child I knew it was a rare honour. Campaigning was gearing up for the presidential elections, which would be held the following month. Karzai rarely left his compound, knowing that the extremists were angered by any display of democracy. This was the first time he had left Kabul since the date of the vote was announced. At last, I heard a distant sound over the mountaintops, something like an angry insect. We all turned our faces to the sky and the sound turned into a loud bass throb as Karzai's helicopter circled like a huge bird over us then began to descend carefully, lower, lower. The wind churned up by the blades pulled at the loose fabric of my coat. Then suddenly there was a huge bang and the sound of shots being fired. I jerked my eyes away from the helicopter, towards the teachers and the soldiers in the field. They all looked shocked; something unplanned was happening. The helicopter stopped its slow descent and reversed upwards quickly, disappearing to a tiny black dot over the mountains. As the roar of its engines retreated, the sound was replaced by frantic shouts and gunfire. The teachers screamed at us to run.

Militants hiding in an abandoned house had fired a rocket at the helicopter, one of several assassination attempts Karzai would survive as president. The rocket missed, and crashed harmlessly into the grass close to the boys' school as Karzai was whisked back to Kabul. A few hours after the attack the Taliban claimed responsibility.

I was furious – at Karzai.

Why did he let that put him off? I fumed.

I had spent hours sweating in the sun waiting to see him. Didn't he know that we all faced that kind of danger every day?

As it turned out, I got the chance to ask Karzai himself a year later. I was selected alongside one of my classmates to attend a conference on children's rights in Kabul, where schoolchildren from around the country could speak with the president. It was held at the Amani High School, one of the city's elite institutions, with a grand history stretching back to the 1920s. The school had been founded by Germans and most classes were taught in that language. It was only during the Taliban's brief tenure that it was closed. I was the youngest there, and everyone kept speaking to me as if I were a child, even though I was eleven and easily able to follow everything they were discussing.

I've been schooled even during the Taliban times! I thought. *How can they speak down to me?*

I thrust my hand into the air before Karzai had finished speaking. I was too small to reach above the heads of the others, though, so as soon as he had finished I stood up.

'I have a question!' I said, as the others glared and shushed at me.

But Karzai saw me, and smiled, saying: 'Let her speak!'

I had planned out in my mind what I was going to say. An assistant rushed between the rows and handed me a microphone. I loved how it made my voice boom out and echo between the walls.

'First of all, in our province, the roads to my school have no concrete. Whenever I go to school on rainy days, my clothes become dirty,' I told him.

I could feel a stunned hush around me. *First?* They were thinking. How many questions does this impertinent kid have?

I continued, not caring a bit for the eyes boring into me.

'Secondly, we don't have English or computer classes for girls in my province. Thirdly, you were planning to come to Paktia. Your helicopter was about to land but you left. I was one of the students who'd waited there all day to welcome you. Why did you leave?'

There are many things I could criticise Karzai for, from his ideas to his way of doing politics. As an adult, I always felt that he was too close to the Taliban, too ready to appease them if it helped him stay in power. Even as the small child I was, I realised that he was largely ineffective, making lots of great promises but rarely seeing them through. Some people called him 'the mayor of Kabul', a snarky reference to his reluctance to leave the capital and his almost total lack of control over the rest of the country.

But I will give Karzai this – he is a great public speaker, and he had the humility that day to let a child question him. He told me he would see to it that English and computer classes were started, and apologised for keeping me waiting to see him in Paktia. Then he invited me up onto the stage, and gave me 500 Afghani from his pocket. Later, he also sent me a certificate and a medal.

The whole thing was broadcast live on TV. It was my first time speaking to the nation, even though I did not know at the time that it was being broadcast! When I got back to Paktia all my teachers were talking about me, telling me how great it was that I had questioned the president. I was invited to the regional governor's office, where I read aloud for his guests from Kabul. When my father's colleagues discovered that it was Abdul Wasi Ghafari's daughter who had stood up and spoken to Karzai, they were amazed and impressed. I went to the military offices in Paktia, too, to read patriotic poems and sing the national anthem to the officers. For the first time, I felt like my father was really proud of me for my achievements, rather than just loving me because I was his daughter. My mother gave me a huge hug, squeezing the air out of me as she told me how I was far braver than her. From then on, I was always called on to be a part of official events: the girl who had arrived from out of town in strange clothes, now something of a local celebrity. If I could pinpoint the real start of my journey upwards, this was it.

I loved going to school, right from the start. Maybe it was because I was not meant to be there in the Taliban times; something about the defiance of it appealed to the stubborn part of my personality. In appalling circumstances, I excelled in my studies, and I was not concerned about anything other than getting ahead and proving myself. Maybe that is why friendship never came easily to me.

Back in Kabul, at the Naswan-e Rahman Mina girls' school, I had made a friend called Sunita. Her face, much more tanned than mine, looked to me like it was made of burnished gold. Her small mouth and eyes always seemed to be smiling, and I never heard a harsh word come out of her. Every day, after classes, we would walk halfway home together, until the point where my house lay in one direction and hers in another. We would speak about everything: what games we were going to play that evening, which Bollywood films we liked best. The one subject that never came up between us was our ethnicities. Sunita was a Hazara, the main Shia Islam group in Afghanistan, and I am Pashtun, the majority, which is Sunni. Again and again, throughout our history, that alone has been the basis for hatred and bloodshed between our two groups. But although we were vaguely aware of this difference, it was never a topic of much interest for me and Sunita, beyond her teaching me a few words in the Hazara language. As an adult, I have often wondered at what point in their lives so many Afghans learn to hate their countrymen. I make a point of avoiding reference to my ethnicity wherever I can, because to me it is the smallest part of my identity. I am Pashtun, but my first language is Dari, and before anything else I am Afghan, and a woman.

One day, Sunita suddenly stopped coming to school. I had noticed that she had been walking more slowly recently, and getting out of breath quicker. After a few weeks had passed, one of the teachers took me aside and told me that she had cancer. Not long after that, I found out that she had died. I was not used to death at that time. Despite the circumstances of my country I had experienced little direct tragedy, cocooned as I was inside the bubble of my family life. I didn't know how to mourn her, or even to accept the fact that she no longer existed on earth. I still think about her today.

I never made another school friend like Sunita. I had friends in my neighbourhood, and my siblings, of course; our pack grew larger every few years. But my relationship with my brothers and sisters was more like that of a parent to a child. From an early age, I was helping to cook for them, and to clean the house. I felt responsible, often bossing them about. Maybe I carried some of that attitude into school, and the other girls felt I was too pushy, too overbearing to be friends with. There were a couple of exceptions in Paktia. One was Rangeeza Noor, the other girl from my school who was chosen to attend Karzai's conference. She and I are still in touch now, and I think we were drawn together by the fact that we both felt like outsiders. The other was Asma, who was my best friend in my last years at high school. She is now married to a journalist, still living in Afghanistan and in fear for their lives. I am trying everything I can think of to help them get out of the country. Otherwise, it was only years later, when I started meeting other women of the same mindset as me – tough, ambitious women who didn't care about being liked – that I started to make real friends.

*

The extremists liked to play at doublethink, claiming that they never targeted students even as they boasted of their campaign against schools. I can tell you from experience that civilians always suffered from their violence, whether we were the targets or not. The first time I was injured in an attack was in 2005, as I was walking close to my school. Suddenly everything went black. I don't remember noise, or an explosion – just that one moment I was walking, thinking about what lessons I had that day, and the next I was waking up in a hospital bed. A suicide bomber had killed ten people and injured more than thirty, including me. The blast had knocked me off my feet and flung me several metres across the road, even though I was a long way away. I was covered in small cuts and grazes and my bones ached for weeks afterwards, but I was lucky that my injuries were mild. Within a couple of days I had recovered enough to carry on with my day-to-day life.

But after that my father said I should stop going to school; he had decided it was too dangerous. Insurgent attacks had soared, increasing seven-fold across the country between 2005 and 2006. In any case, we would be moving back to Kabul in two years – I could continue with my schooling there. I was devastated. There was no point pleading with him – I could never change his mind like that; instead, I took my chances, doing a reverse bunking-off by sneaking out to school when he went out to work.

I was getting away with it, until the suicide bombers struck again. This time it was September 2006, and again I was walking to school, full of energy and enthusiasm at the start of the new academic year. I was walking down the main street of Gardez, where all the government buildings are. It is one of the most well-guarded areas in the city, always full of roadblocks and soldiers. The governor's armoured car drove past me in a convoy, and pulled up at the gates of his office. I still remember how beautiful those gates were, ornate metalwork varnished in bright colours. Then another car turned into the square ahead of me, about a hundred metres away. *That's not right*, I thought. All the roads had been blocked off to normal traffic. This time I heard the sound, a huge blast that seemed to blow in my eardrums at the same time as all the air was sucked out of my lungs. I remember flying backwards, and hitting the ground, then everything else was a blank.

The Taliban had killed Hakim Taniwal, the governor of Paktia. It was their biggest attack in the region to date, and they had chosen their target deliberately. This was the first time they had managed to kill a provincial governor, and Taniwal was a scholar, a professor of sociology who had fled the bigotry of the mujahideen in 1979 and built a life in exile in Australia. He returned to Afghanistan in 2002, leaving behind his worried family and vowing to do everything he could to help rebuild his homeland. In a series of government postings in eastern Afghanistan, he worked hard to bring the squabbling tribes together and fight against endemic corruption. He was known by almost everyone as a good, honest man.

I don't know whether the strange car I saw just before the explosion actually had anything to do with it: a suicide bomber on foot had thrown himself under Taniwal's car, killing him, his nephew, his driver and his bodyguard. But the timing of the attack was no coincidence. Only days earlier Pervez Musharraf, the Pakistani prime minister, had made an agreement with the Taliban-supporting tribes in the border regions abutting Paktia. Taniwal had openly criticised the deal, warning that Pakistan was giving the militants carte blanche to cross the border into Afghanistan. The slaughter heralded the start of a new era of violence. A day later, at Taniwal's funeral, another suicide bomber killed six more people.

When I opened my eyes I knew nothing of this – only that I was in so much pain. The impact of the blast had fractured my skull in three places, and my face and hands were bandaged. Shrapnel had gouged chunks out of my skin. As my vision cleared I realised that I was in a hospital, and that my parents were sitting beside my bed.

'You'll be fine, don't worry,' said my mother, repeating it over and over as tears streamed down her face.

My father, though, was dry-eyed and grim. The first words he said to me were: 'See, I told you this would happen.'

Of course he was worried about me, and inside he was crying as hard as my mother. But Afghan men do not show their emotions. He was also furious with me for disobeying his instructions. Straight away, he started talking again about how I would not be going to school in Paktia any more, how I was young, and that taking a couple of years off wouldn't matter. I could only listen, too groggy to argue back, the pain in my heart more acute than anything I was feeling on my body. I could not bear the thought of not going to school. At that time I was still determined to become an ambassador, and to do that I had to pass my exams and go to university. I feared that the short break from school my father was proposing would turn into a permanent rupture; that the militants' attacks were going to keep escalating, that there would always be a reason for me not to return to my classes. Even as I lay there in hospital, my mind was whirring, coming up with ways to defy my father once more.

The doctors told me that my wounds would heal, despite the agony I was in. Again, I had been lucky. I was discharged after one night, with an order to rest at home. As soon as I settled down onto a cushion in our house I began plotting how I might sneak out to school again. I knew that from then on I would have to make it seem as if I had been at home all day. So, I waited until my parents had gone to work and then rushed to my classes, usually getting there a little bit late. Towards the end of the school day I would tell my teacher I had to get back home to look after my brothers and sisters, and I would hurry back home to be there when my dad got in. It was all working out perfectly until my father caught me again. This time, his rage was volcanic. He beat me with a belt until my body ached. To this day, I cannot stand seeing such violence, even when it is just on television.

I cannot blame my father. As tough as he was, he too was scared of what other men might say about him if he allowed me to live my dreams freely. And he was scared that the next time there was an attack I might not survive. Moreover, in his years fighting the mujahideen he had seen the dangers that awaited women when they stepped out-side, away from home. By the time I was born, Afghanistan had endured two decades of turmoil that had twisted its beautiful culture into something perverse.

Afghanistan's original Islamic traditions are a lively mix. Around a quarter of the population are Shia, and most of the rest practise the Hanafi version of Sunniism, which offers one of the most liberal interpretations of the holy texts. Sufism, a mystical form of Islam that elevates rituals and music and poetry, also has a long history in Afghanistan and has played a huge part in shaping its culture.

But the radical Islamism that later spread to Afghanistan emerged in India in the late nineteenth century, when the country was still part of the British empire and its population included a large number of Muslims. The Deobandi tradition, a harsh, unbending interpretation of Islam, sprang from within the Hanafi movement, and was also influenced by Sufism, but it took its interpretations in a radical new direction. The Deobandi leaders merged a strict interpretation of the Quran with anti-colonialist politics, producing a kind of Islamic evangelicalism. It took off quickly, particularly among the Pashtun tribes, and when Pakistan split from India in 1947 most Deobandi scholars moved there. After that, global politics intervened. The Soviet invasion of Afghanistan prompted the CIA to fund armed groups made up of fighters who had studied in the Pakistani madrassas, and Saudi Arabia used its wealth and influence to push Wahhabism, an even more extreme interpretation of Islam.

While the West was undergoing a social revolution that brought with it a host of new rights for women – the contraceptive pill, equal pay, the right to abortion – in Afghanistan, 90 per cent of women remained illiterate and the rising religious ideologues made sure it stayed that way. Under the mujahideen and then the Taliban, the mullahs – the men of religion – rose to high positions of social power. How does one become a mullah? By devoting a lifetime to studying the Quran, Islamic theology and law. But in Afghanistan since the rise of the fanatics, most powerful mullahs have been trained in the madrassas of Pakistan, where they are schooled in the Deobandi tradition. One single seminary, the Darul Uloom Haqqania in Pakistan's Khyber province, close to the Afghan border, has educated more Taliban leaders than any other place and bestowed an honorary doctorate on the co-founder and first leader of the Taliban, Mullah Omar.

In Afghanistan, the mullahs took Islam and shaped it to suit themselves.

As I grew up, I began to understand the position of women in Afghanistan bit by bit, pieces of a jigsaw slotting into place. In Kabul, during the Taliban's reign, a blue burka hung from a peg by the front door, so that my mother would throw it over herself whenever she stepped out, as natural a part of her ritual as putting on her shoes. And when I was around six years old, I saw the bogeymen for the first time. I was walking to the communal water pump in Kart-e Naw, close to the neighbourhood mosque, when I spotted a bundle of dirty white cloth on the pavement. It was cowering beneath a man who was bringing down a whip, over and over and over. I froze in my spot and watched, knowing that something terrible was happening in front of me. It took me some moments to realise that the bundle was a woman. The Taliban fighter was whipping her feet – her crime may have been showing her ankles because her burka was too short, or that she had neglected to wear socks with her sandals. Under the Taliban's interpretations, even the sole of a woman's foot could be sexualised. As I stood there I realised that she was screaming. Only when the beating stopped and she stood up and ran away did I snap back to reality. Tiny as I was, I knew this treatment might lie in store for me, too.

Even without the threat of such public punishments meted out by religious fanatics, women in my country are always controlled, penned in by social mores that are policed by everyone. Afghan men are terrible gossips. They gossip in front of the mosque after they have just prostrated themselves to Allah, they gossip in the tea shops while chain-smoking cigarettes, and they gossip in the store as the attendant weighs out their vegetables. The subject of their conversations? Women. Who has allowed their wife to go to the market? Whose young daughter has been seen playing with boys? To have a woman in the family who is in charge of her own life is a source of shame for a man in Afghanistan, a sign that he is not strong enough to keep his female charges in line. When Afghan men fight each other, their first recourse is to curse each other's wives, mothers, sisters, even daughters.

One of my earliest memories from our house in Kabul was when some of my father's friends were visiting and I – six years old, head uncovered, full of confidence and noise – wanted to sit with them. But it was my younger brother who got to take the tea in to the adults. I was not allowed into the room. I was around the same age when my father brought me a huge jar of marbles. I was so good at that game – I would always beat the boys of my age in my neighbourhood. But in Afghanistan, they say that marbles is not a game for girls, that we should be playing instead with dolls and learning how to clean and cook. Some of our neighbours had seen me, and told my dad that I had been hanging around with the boys. After that, he forbade me from playing with them on my own. But sometimes, when he was around, he would take me and my brothers out himself. As long as he was watching me, I was allowed to play with boys my own age.

From the time I became a teenager, I could never leave my house in Kabul without enduring endless comments from teenage boys. When I wore the panjabi, a loose, Indian-style tunic, over my trousers, they would say that the slits at the side went too far up. 'Look, we can see her back!' I would hear from behind me as I boarded the bus. When I wore my headscarf tight around my face, they would say I must be a mullah. I consciously went through a list of different outfits, trying a new style each day to see which one would keep them quiet. None of them did, of course – those little fashion critics, Afghanistan's own Gianni Versaces, had a snide comment to make about whatever I wore. Mostly, I just wore jeans, which I felt most comfortable in.

'Oh, welcome to Europe!' they would jeer.

But what were they wearing? They were also in jeans, generally so ill-fitting they showed half of their backsides.

They didn't even have respect for my mother, who always wore a long, modest coat when she left the house. One day, we went together to the mall to buy perfume and a group of teenage boys started shouting at us.

'Look,' said one of them, laughing, 'the elder is more beautiful!'

All this in the most cosmopolitan city in the country, during a time of relative security and freedom. Eventually, I stopped trying to appease them. If I was going to change things in my country, then what men thought of my appearance had to be the least of my worries.

Three

Kabul is one of those places that squeezes your heart. I don't say this because it is my city – it is an objective truth. Plenty of outsiders will back me up. Look at a map of Central Asia, aim your finger at the dead centre, and you will hit somewhere close to Kabul. It is about as far from the sea as it is possible to be in this part of the world, its inaccessibility part of its fascination. It is elevated more than a mile above sea level, and surrounded by the majestic mountain ranges of the Hindu Kush. To the north-east is the Koh-e Shirdarwaza, or Lion Gate Mountain, bisected by the old city walls that are said to include human bones in their bricks; to the south-west is Koh-e Qrough; and to the east is Koh-e Paghman, nicknamed 'the stony girdle' – together, they gather around Kabul, an embrace against the outside world. To even get as far as its mountain gates, you must cross some difficult terrain. From Pakistan, to the south-east, you must traverse the legendary Khyber Pass, a route through mountain territory where tribal law still rules. To the west, much of the border with Iran cuts through unforgiving desert. To the north, the scenery is more verdant, but good luck getting visas to cross into Afghanistan from Turkmenistan, Tajikistan or Uzbekistan.

Before war corrupted my country, it was a place that tourists visited, a fabled stop-off on the Hippie Trail to India. The last echoes of that era still ring out on Chicken Street, a garbled parade of curio shops which runs north of the Kabul river. Here you can buy rugs with machine gun designs woven into them, battered bronze keepsakes, sumptuous jewellery studded with precious lapis lazuli, a deep purple stone found in the limestone mountains of north-eastern Afghanistan, and old postcards from the time when Kabul was a swinging city. Around another narrow corner you'll find the bird market, full of gloriously plumed partridges and peacocks that Afghans keep as pampered pets. Just outside the city limits the landscape opens up into dramatic vistas painted in jewel-like colours. Families picnic by the Qargha reservoir, a pleasure lake just outside the city where a line of vendors sell *shor nakhod*, a spicy chickpea soup, from their wagons. In spring the cherry blossom turns whole swathes of the mountainsides to pink. In the evenings flocks of white doves descend as if out of nowhere onto the city pavements, and on summer nights the air in the outer suburbs is filled with the sound of cicadas. In the daytime, locals joke and barter in their thick Kabuli accents, their vowel sounds plump with joy.

Kabul's appeal has little to do with its amenities. The rubbish often goes uncollected, and the Kabul river has long since dried up into a crusty stream. Shopkeepers are not bothered by aesthetics: their signs tend to assault your eyeballs with neon and clashing colour schemes, and their shop windows are generally grimy and cluttered. If a brand or proprietor wants to prove the quality of his wares, he attaches the word 'Turkish' to his business name – Turkey is seen as the fountain of everything well-made and stylish. The smaller roads on the outskirts are still unpaved, and acrid diesel-fuel traffic fumes hang over everything. Newcomers often hang their washing out on their balconies when they first arrive from the villages, but quickly realise that their whites turn grey when they do.

You have to search a little to find Kabul's beauty – that's part of its charm. You will catch a glimpse of it on a crisp winter day, when the gleaming sun makes the snow on the mountaintops glisten. You will hear it in the frantic electronic music leaking from the stores that sell bootleg CDs, and the calls of the men selling potatoes, onions, tomatoes and peppers that they've harvested from the gardens they tend at home, a rainbow of produce laid out on blue tarpaulin at the roadside. You will see it in the contrasts – in the brightly coloured rugs slung over the saddles of the donkeys trotting alongside luxury SUVs, and the silhouettes of the palaces against the pale blue sky: Darul Aman, the folly of a twentieth-century king, in the south of the city, and the ancient fortress of Bala Hissar perched above it. Drive on the mountain road out of the city, and you are rewarded with a panoramic cityscape that gradually reveals itself as you climb. By day, the jumble of buildings down below looks like a living mosaic; by night, the city lights make it seem like a galaxy seen from above. Back down in the streets, remnants of a once vibrant city jump out at you, a reminder of what

74

Kabul used to be: an exquisitely carved marble fountain that hasn't gurgled with water for decades; the last pieces of a mosaic clinging to a façade; the decaying shell of a mansion revealed behind warped wooden doors; an overgrown bougainvillea in full bloom, the survivor of a once-manicured garden. Street cameramen, with their box Brownies, capture something of the essence when they take your portrait. No matter how still you stand, there is always an extra outline around you like an aura, the imperfection that makes the image sublime.

With the arrival of the foreigners in 2001, Kabul added a ring of protection around its vital organs, huge slabs of concrete topped with barbed wire that ringed public buildings and upmarket hotels. The parliament, the presidential palace, the central bank and the embassies disappeared behind concrete blocks, and those areas became off-limits for ordinary people. Tree-lined boulevards that had once been used for evening strolls became unnavigable by foot. Gradually people walked less, and became more reliant on buses and cars. The braver men cycled, weaving through the lawless traffic, sometimes with a tiny child clinging onto their back.

Nothing stays unadorned for long in Kabul. These blank concrete canvases inspired a generation of graffiti artists, who took the city's troubles as their subject matter and turned it into something beautiful. Flowers, women's faces, birds and calligraphed slogans, calls for peace alongside cartoons making fun of the politicians, Banksy-style stencils and dream-like montages – against the grey and grime of the pavements, these artworks were windows into the soul of Kabul. The rickshaws too, the very cheapest public transport, were flying jewels of coloured metal, done out like gypsy caravans.

My love for my home city really blossomed when we returned to Kabul from Paktia in 2009, when I was fifteen years old. I was seeing it through adult eyes for the first time, as not just a jumble of identikit buildings, but a place with a human soul. After the beige of the Paktia Badlands, the buzz of the big city enveloped me: the mix of people, the diversity of faces. With the Taliban gone, Kabulis' real character had emerged once more: foul-mouthed, sometimes aggressive, but always with a quick smile, a ready joke, and a willingness to help out anyone in trouble. For me, though, this was also a dark time. I had sat my university entrance exam just before we left Paktia, and I had done well enough to win a place to study law at Khost province's Sheikh Zayed University, one of the newest and best institutions in the country.

Although my father had allowed and even encouraged me to sit the exam, I knew before I broached the subject that he would not allow me to attend that university. Khost also borders Pakistan and had become a hotbed of the Taliban insurgency. Moreover, allowing his daughter to live alone would be unthinkable. That day, once again, I simply listened without arguing back. I was worn down and couldn't say a word; all I could do was cry. For years I had been agreeing to his restrictions and then finding my own way around them. This time I felt that my dreams had died. I had earned a place at university, studied hard, never giving him any reason to be ashamed. Yet still he was stopping me, not because he thought I was doing the wrong thing but because he didn't want the other men to gossip about him. It was hopeless. Was I to be just another Afghan woman whose job was to clean and have children? My life stretched before me, all the work I had done for nothing. I had always respected my father, but I wondered why he was causing me such pain. I had done everything that a family in another part of the world would want from their daughter, but in Afghanistan that seemed to be a source of shame. For the first time, I felt an uneasy notion creeping over me: the realisation that I could never be accepted in my home country.

For a teenager this was a lot to take in. It went beyond just feeling different to my peers: it was a sense of utter alienation from everything and everyone I knew, a hollowness in my chest that I could no longer ignore. I tried to quash it by squeezing my eyes tight shut and hugging myself, crying until I had nothing left. But once I was done crying, I still felt raw. I ripped up every single one of my certificates, including my exam grades and the one Karzai had given me, weeping as the thick paper tore between my fingers. Then I searched in my mother's cleaning cupboard for something that would kill me. I half remembered warnings from my mother about which ones were dangerous, but the jumble of labels was blurred behind the tears that were filling my eyes. I clutched at the nearest one, wincing at its sourness as it slipped down my throat, and then closed my eyes, convinced this would be the end. Fortunately, what I had grabbed was watered-down detergent, nothing strong enough to do me any real harm. When I woke up the next morning, apparently unaffected, I was disappointed at first. Even death had been taken from me! But as I lay there, fuming, I started to feel ridiculous.

My father had stopped me for now but he couldn't hold me back from university for ever. He had married an educated woman, after all, and even during the darkest days of our relationship I somehow knew that he did want me to become something more than what our society expected. I feel sympathy for him now, more than anger; he was caught in an impossible position. In the time since he was taken from me, my feelings have turned to gratitude: I don't think I would have become the person I am today if he hadn't been so hard on me.

Back in Kabul, I sat in the house, eaten up with anger at the fact that I wasn't now establishing a new life on campus, meeting friends and delving into books. I could have taken up a place at Kabul University – my father would have allowed that, since I would have carried on living at home. But my stubborn character meant I felt that such a compromise would be a failure, indicating that I was happy with my father controlling my choices when in fact I was enraged. But I soon got bored with my life without school; all I did was clean, cook and go to the market. I was at the age when everyone asked when I was going to get married, whether it was their business or not. I hadn't even considered such a thing; I had never met a single Afghan man who I thought I could have lived with for more than a day. Meanwhile my younger brothers were out enjoying their freedom. They were preparing for their own university entrance exams now – how unfair it would be if they went before me!

One day I had an idea: maybe I could work as a teacher at the school my sisters were attending. I asked my father whether he would allow it, and for once he agreed. This was a private girls' school, and I caught the bus there with my sisters every day. There was absolutely nothing anyone could gossip about – it was a respectable job for an educated woman in Kabul. In Afghanistan, a 'respectable job' is restricted to doctor or teacher, although most men would prefer that their wives just work in the house. I taught English and mathematics and at the same time I secretly enrolled in an English course myself. I knew the language already but wanted to improve, to reach a level that would take me around the world. I had still not given up on my dream of being a diplomat, rubbing shoulders with top politicians and influencing the big issues of the day. I was watching them on television every day now, my hunger for world events fed through the television, my sole link to places outside Afghanistan. They all seemed so impressive, so assured when they spoke at summits and in interviews. To become a diplomat, my English had to be flawless. I was meant to give all my salary to the household budget, but I told my father that I was being paid less than I actually was and used the difference to pay for my course at a private language school. There, in snatched hours, I started reading novels in English, gradually getting used to the flow of letters on the page until I got to a point where I could just enjoy the literature, no longer battling with the language.

My lucky break came when I had just turned sixteen, through a chance encounter at the education ministry, where I had gone to pick up a document for one of my colleagues as a favour. As I was waiting at the ministry, one of the bureaucrats there, curious about my background, asked what I was doing with my life. I told him that I was working as a teacher, but that I really dreamed of working in a high public office. I recounted how I had passed my university entrance exams but had been unable to take up my place. He seemed interested, I noticed, but thought nothing more of it when I walked out the door. When I returned to the ministry on another errand a few weeks later, however, a group of officials spotted me and called me over. One of them was a member of parliament and, to my surprise, he knew my name. The official I had first spoken to had already told him my story. The government of India was offering scholarships to Afghan girls, he said, and he thought I would be a perfect candidate.

That little flame inside me sparked up again. In an instant, I felt all the ambitions I had been pushing down re-emerging. Someone had spotted potential in me, and now I was able to imagine my future again. India! I felt I had already been there, even though I had never left Afghanistan. I had loved Bollywood films ever since my father brought that first video back from the shop to play on our new colour TV. In that place, where women in miniskirts danced in the street, I would be free from all the petty gossip and vindictiveness that was keeping me confined. I would be away from the gaze of Afghan men, no longer caring what they thought.

My mother privately agreed with me: this would be the best opportunity of my life. But she couldn't go against the wishes of my father. First, we had to persuade him, but at least this time I had an ally. Together we planned how we should approach him: strength in numbers would be the best tactic. We called my aunt in Germany, rallied my mother's cousin and two of my maternal uncles, including my favourite, whom I called Haji Muma. Together, the four of them sat down with my father, with my aunt on the phone from Germany, while I sat in the next room, listening through the wall. At first, he gave the same response I had heard so many times:

'No, it's not possible. I won't allow it.'

But they pressed on, in a way I had never been able to on my own. My mother said I had earned this opportunity, with everything that I had suffered in going to school. My aunt said that in a modern society girls should have the same right to education as boys, and if they did not then Afghanistan would never progress. My uncle told him that I had behaved impeccably my entire life, and there was no reason to think I would behave differently in India. Suddenly, my father cracked:

'I don't care, then, do what you want!'

My scholarship won me a place at the Panjab University in Chandigarh, a small city in northern India. I started there in the autumn of 2010, the first time I had ever left Afghanistan. After years of watching Bollywood films I was sure that I knew what awaited me, and that I would be able to fit straight in. But the contrast with chaotic, grimy Kabul was so startling it took me a few weeks to adjust – even to the climate. The sun was scorching, but its rays softened through layers of cloud and humidity. It rained often – not with the sparse, brief showers that fall on Kabul but with thunderous downpours that turned streets into rivers and stopped as abruptly as they started.

Moreover, the rainwater did not linger and stagnate as it would in an Afghan city. Here, it was whisked away by an efficient drainage system, and once the sun re-emerged the pavements would dry within minutes.

My senses were overwhelmed on my first day. There was the heady sweetness of the flowers on the side of the roads, their petals opening up after the rain to release their scent into the air. There was the clamorous sound of people talking in high-pitched melodious Hindi, a language I did not understand. And there was the sight of men and women mixing together freely, the women showing more skin than I had ever seen, and walking in strong strides with their heads held high.

Despite this, at the start, I was homesick. I found myself clinging to parts of my own culture. I began wearing my headscarf tight to my face, rather than the loose arrangement I had preferred in Kabul, when I had bothered to wear it at all. Initially the people in my classes assumed I was a strict Muslim and were hesitant to speak with me. I was also nervous about my English. I was at a far lower level than I had thought in Kabul, where I was always top of my class – and this was the language I was going to be studying in. When I brought home the books for the courses I had chosen – economics, political science and public administration – I flicked through the fat wedges of pages and gazed distraught at the closely packed text. How would I even begin to read this, let alone understand it? For a week the books sat on my desk as I stared at them, too scared to even open a page. I was so consumed by the fear of gossip that an Afghan upbringing had embedded in me that I did not want to tell anyone else my concerns, lest they go and tell others that I was not fit to be here. The girls whom I was sharing a flat with, Afghans on scholarships like me, reminded me immediately of the older girls who had always excluded me from their friendship groups at school. Again I was the youngest, just sixteen. On our first day together all my fears overwhelmed me and I sat silently on my suitcase as they chatted and laughed.

Maybe they're talking about me, I wondered.

After few minutes I gathered up the courage to ask the other girls what subjects they were taking.

'We don't know,' one of them said. 'All we know is that this is our house.'

I had come all the way from Afghanistan for this?

My mother had packed me a suitcase full of tea, milk, rice and other things that she must have thought I would not be able to find easily in India. There were also plates, cutlery, cups, toiletries – it was as if I were carrying a small house with me. None of it soothed me in those early weeks. But as it turned out, the girls I was living with in the university flat were totally different from the bullies and cliques I had encountered at school. They weren't gossiping about me at all on that first day – I had just become used to being the odd one out. Now, for the first time in my life, I felt like I actually fitted in. Yet all I could think of was the cosy familiarity of the life I had left behind, despite its traumas and struggles.

I had thought the women in my family at least would be proud of me once my father finally gave in and I took up my scholarship. But on the morning of my flight to India, my maternal grandmother dealt me a crueller blow than my father ever had. I had gone to her house to say goodbye – until that morning I had not told her that I was leaving. But when I went to kiss her hand, a traditional show of respect and love for older relatives in Afghanistan, she pulled it away and turned her head to the wall. After a few seconds of awful silence she began cursing me, calling me a disgrace who was bringing shame on my family and abandoning my mother to pursue my own wild dreams. She carried on, her voice growing louder in front of other guests as she asked them what they thought of my mother allowing me to go. Eventually I couldn't bear it any more – I left the room without saying the proper goodbye to my grandmother, shaking with a sick feeling in my belly.

Outside, I found my mother crying. 'It's because you're going so far away,' she told me.

Infuriated, I went back into the room where my grandmother was sitting. She was telling the guests how my parents were allowing me to go to university overseas – an unthinkable thing in her eyes. I love my grandmother deeply, and respect her. And I know she loves me too, a lot. It burned me to know that she was so angry. But I also couldn't bear to hear her criticise my mother. Something rose up inside me, overwhelming all the family and social codes that command you to defer to your elders.

'Don't talk about her like that!' I said.

My grandmother couldn't believe my nerve. 'Who are you to interrupt me?' she retorted. 'She's my daughter!'

'Well,' I replied, the guests wide-eyed now, and silent. 'If she's your daughter then I am hers. And I can't stay in a place where my mother is being disrespected.'

I turned and walked out of the room, back to where my

mother was crying. My aunties and cousin were running after me by now, begging me to stop and have breakfast at least. It was too late. I could not eat a mouthful. Even by the time I boarded the plane hours later, a nausea remained within me. I had never had such an argument with my grandmother.

In Chandigarh I pushed my ugly departure to the back of my mind and told myself that everything would be better when I went home to visit. They all would have missed me, and with time and space they would forgive me, maybe even start to feel proud. But when I returned to Kabul for the first time, seven months after I had left, I felt as if a curtain had fallen between us. My father acted as though he hardly knew me. He barely spoke a word to me, and I could not even catch his eye over dinner. I was sure that, at some point, he would call me *Sartajak*, or that we would crack one of our in-jokes, and then he would laugh and everything would be normal again. But he did not. Each night in Kabul I cried myself to sleep and after several days I decided to return to India sooner than I had planned.

Chandigarh was designed by architect Charles-Édouard Jeanneret (more famously known as Le Corbusier) to be a perfectly planned modernist idyll, its buildings experiments in concrete form and function, and was created in 1949, after the violently contentious division of India that led to the formation of the country of Pakistan. Jawaharlal Nehru, the Indian prime minister who commissioned Chandigarh, wanted it to be a symbol of peace and democracy and it is probably the city that comes closest to realising the modernists' dream. Its roads are wide and well-paved, botanic gardens scattered throughout, and just outside the city, at the Shivalik foothills, sits Sukhna lake, created especially for the city's residents to enjoy. Le Corbusier's and Nehru's dream has been realised – Chandigarh has been named repeatedly as the happiest city in India, and one of the best places in the world to live.

Despite my difficult start, after a few weeks I started loving my life in Chandigarh. The walls of my own mental prison started crumbling, my eyes opening up a little more each day. The first lecture had me hooked on economics within five minutes. I loved how it applied mathematical concepts to society, a perfect fusion of politics and mathematics, my two favourite subjects at school. I also realised that my English was good enough to do the course, after all. Moreover, I was now meeting new people from different countries every day and speaking with them in English, our common language. It was the first time that nobody commented about my age, or tried to take advantage of me because of it. After classes we would go together to a café and eat *golgappa*, a deep-fried, ball-shaped crispy snack filled with vegetables coated in a thin, spicy sauce. You can't nibble on it politely – the sauce spills down your chin. You have to push the whole thing into your mouth in one go and feel the satisfying pop as you sink your teeth into it and it explodes. There were boys and girls together: laughing, talking and treating each other as equals. If I was having a fun conversation with someone, he did not try to twist it – it just meant that we were friends. It took me a few weeks to stop double-guessing what others might be assuming of me every time I said something to a man.

But once I did, I felt liberated. I realised that in this place nobody else really much cared what other people were doing with their lives. They were just minding their own business, respecting the right of everyone to choose their own path. Of course India has its own problems, and women are certainly not living in a paradise there. Most of the country is still deeply patriarchal and suffers horrific rates of domestic violence, sexual abuse and femicide – to counter this, they have a strong feminist movement. But in happy, wealthy Chandigarh, among my liberal university friends, I felt safe and valued as a woman for the first time in my life.

When I arrived in India I didn't have any money for new clothes, so I continued wearing my Afghan outfits, mostly long dresses stitched with intricate patterns. Gradually, though, I began experimenting with different styles. I bought a long blazer in green and purple silk that I wore with black trousers and ballet pumps. I started wearing colourful panjabis over billowing trousers and, most daring of all, I tried the outfits the other college girls looked so comfortable in: jeans, T-shirts, blazers. It was a revelation. I felt free to move, no longer consumed with worries about what might be showing or what I might trip over. I made a group of solid friends, the best of them being Babita, from Nepal. She and I practised different religions – she was Buddhist – yet I soon found that we had more in common than I had with any of the girls I'd gone to school with in Afghanistan. Babita and I would walk around the city for hours together, talking about whatever was in our heads and laughing until the tears leaked from our eyes. Through her I met her cousin, Puja, who was younger than us but also great fun, and a whole group of other girls. When we sat together I would take off my scarf and realise that not only did we look similar, we were like-minded. When Babita was married in Kolkata, we all travelled down there for the wedding party. It went on for days, with men and women dancing together and outfits covered in dazzling jewels. I came away determined that, when I got married, it would be a mixed ceremony and that I would wear the most stunning outfit I could find.

Life in my country had already left its marks on my body before I arrived in India. You are probably wondering how I felt about being injured in terror attacks twice before I was even an adult. Here is the truth: emotionally, I blocked those things out. If you are reading this in a safe country, where a single atrocity will make the news headlines for days or weeks afterwards, you may not be able to imagine how a country like Afghanistan deals with its horrors. Here's how: it clears up and carries on, and does nothing to deal with the trauma. An explosion might kill dozens and destroy a school or a mosque, or an airstrike might turn a home into a crater and wipe the whole family out. But the next day, people will be walking past there again and nobody will comment on what happened, despite the stray shards of glass underfoot and faint smell of charcoal in the air. If we lingered too long, then we would never have time for anything other than our grief, and so we push it right down inside us, and convince ourselves that this has become our normal. But it never really does become normal. Each attack ripped jagged holes in our collective psyche, the same way they do in your country. Every person killed or injured had, until the millisecond before the detonator sparked the explosives, been thinking about what they might have for dinner that evening, or a girl in the neighbourhood they liked the look of. In my case, both times I was caught up in a bombing, I had been thinking about what I was going to study at school that day, and then in an instant of blinding light and heat, a vacuum blast pulled the air out of me, threw me backwards, and sucked those thoughts of school into the void. When I came to, and realised what I had survived, I knew that nobody was going to comment on it much. Surviving a terror attack – even two – did not make me special or even interesting. It made me Afghan, at a time when violence was what our country did best.

It was the dissonance of being hurt in India that made my next accident so much more traumatic, even though, this time, nobody had set out to hurt me. Two years into my degree, I had lost my innate distrust of my surroundings. It felt like nothing bad or even unplanned could happen in this smooth, functional city – although, of course, terrible things can happen anywhere. Again, I was thinking about my studies as misfortune hit, hurrying out of the university library with an armful of economics textbooks one evening as the sun was creeping down below the horizon. I was so consumed by my thoughts that I did not realise I was stepping out into the road, nor hear the car speeding towards me. I do not even remember the last moments before impact; witnesses told me that the car sent my body flying.

This time, my injuries were serious. I was in a coma for twenty-five days, and the doctors gave me a 1 per cent chance of survival. Even when I came round, the right side of my body was paralysed, and it was only weeks later that feeling and movement started coming back. Of all the traumas I had suffered to date, this was the one that left the most physical scarring: a pebbledash of wounds on the side of my face, and half of my teeth knocked out. Bones all over my body were cracked and broken, and I have never moved with the same ease since. When I look at photos of myself before that accident, my face seems young and full. The accident aged me years in the space of a couple of months.

My mother came from Kabul to my bedside. It was her face I saw first when I woke, just as it had been when I was injured in the attacks in Paktia. One of my uncles had come with her, and at first I was grateful to him, and happy that she was not there on her own. But later I learnt that he had taken it upon himself to start investigating my life in India, while I was still lying unconscious. Instead of sitting with my distraught mother by my bedside he had wandered all over the city, asking whether I had been drunk, or if I had been coming from a party, or with a man when the accident happened. When he found nothing scandalous, he called my grandmother.

'Do you remember when you cursed at her?' he asked. 'She's been living a good life. Everyone talks nicely about her. I'm so proud of her, and you should be, too.'

He may have been proud, but I was livid when my friends told me the questions he had been asking. He cared more about these things than about my life and health, even as I was lying unconscious? That incident reaffirmed for me that what Afghan men call honour is actually a sickness in their minds. I did not speak with my uncle for several days.

The strength I found to overcome my injuries and my rage at my uncle's prejudices was undoubtedly rooted in the independence I had in India. It was as if my personality was filling out. I was developing into myself, a person I was proud of, yet I hardly went wild in Chandigarh: I studied hard, I went to cafés with my friends, and sometimes I sat by myself at the edge of Sukhna lake, music playing in my headphones as I cried for my country and the people I missed. I did not drink and never went to clubs and bars. All I wanted was to learn as much about the world as I could, and get the best education possible. A stroke of luck had brought me here, to one of the best public universities in India, and I was not going to let these opportunities go.

After three years of hard work, aged nineteen and growing up far from my family, I completed my bachelor's degree. I knew I was not yet finished, and signed up immediately for the master's course, another two years on full scholarship. My physical distance from my family did not make me love them any less, but it did make me less concerned about their reaction. Of course, my mother told me that she missed me and wished that I would come back to Kabul – but if she hadn't said that, then she wouldn't have done her duty as an Afghan mother. Underneath her words, I felt her willing me to carry on. Without her help I would never have arrived here, and I knew that she would have absorbed much of the extended family's disapproval towards me. Meanwhile I threw myself into student life and politics, part of the tradition at Panjab University. I joined the student union, and was voted in as the Panjab University student council representative for foreign students. By the time I left India I was nearly twenty-two years old, an adult, with my mind and eyes opened. I was ready to go back to my country and serve it, as had been my intention all along.

Was there one moment when I became a feminist, or decided that I should dedicate my life to working for women's rights? It was more of a steady build, made up of moments when I could barely contain my fury at the injustices my society was doling out to me. Every time a boy patronised me, tried unsolicited to explain something to me that I understood very well already, I felt another scream mounting inside. As I grew up, I started to realise that my body was a problem that I was expected to mitigate, despite the fact that it was men who were behaving badly towards it. The tipping point came with the death of Farkhunda Malikzada, a 27-year-old woman who was lynched by a mob on a Kabul street on 19 March 2015, during my last year in Chandigarh. I saw the whole thing on Facebook. Her murderers were brazen, arrogant and so sure of their righteousness that they had filmed the lynching, and posted their videos online.

Farkhunda had been visiting the Shah-Do Shamshira mosque, a beautiful baroque building in the old city, on the bank of the Kabul river. There, she argued with a group of men who were selling amulets, Viagra and condoms – an insult to the faith of which Farkhunda was a knowledgeable student. The men, enraged at being corrected by a woman, went into the street and shouted that Farkhunda had burnt a Quran inside the shrine. Within seconds, a mob gathered. They started beating her with sticks and shoes, continuing even as she fell to the ground. They dragged her for 300 metres, and then called on the driver of a car to run her over. Her headscarf had been ripped off and her clothes were in tatters. Those who were not joining in her torture were filming it.

The video went viral, capturing a ghoulish zeitgeist and giving voice to the mounting sense of dismay many Afghan women were feeling. We had been promised something so different when the Americans landed in 2001: the end of the Taliban; the flowering of democracy; equal rights. So why, in 2015, with the Taliban apparently long gone, were we seeing such a barbaric and public act of violence against an innocent woman, falsely accused? Afghanistan was still stuck in the era where they burned witches. From my apartment in India, in a more modern world, I watched those videos and wept.

I had rewired parts of my personality in the years that I had spent away from Afghanistan, but I couldn't break the bonds that tied me to my homeland. I had to do something, and started telling my university friends about what had happened to Farkhunda, watching the expression in their eyes turn from curiosity to horror. I had told them snippets about women's lives in my country, but usually I told them about the better side of Afghanistan. I am a patriot, and I want people to know how beautiful my country is, to hear about our music and poetry, the mountains and crystal skies. They see enough of its grim side on the news, I reasoned.

This time I did not want to varnish anything for them.

My country is beautiful and its people are kind and dignified, but extremism drags it into the gutter. My quest to tell people in Chandigarh about Farkhunda evolved into a campaign. I started organising protests on campus, calling for justice to be served to her killers. I stood in the middle, in my headscarf and chic outfit, surrounded by classmates, male and female, who had joined my campaign. Together, we started a petition to send to the justice ministry in Afghanistan.

There are many examples of how social media can be used to twist and undermine human rights and democracy, but in this case it worked in our favour. Farkhunda's brutal murder sent waves of revulsion around the world, and our petition became part of a mounting global pressure on the Afghan government to enforce some kind of justice and retribution. They conceded, and investigated the attack; forty-nine people stood trial. Many were found innocent and released, but the four main perpetrators, including the man who had shouted that she was burning the Quran and so triggered the attack, were sentenced to death. The man who posted the video also received the death sentence, as did another who kicked her corpse and removed her clothes.

The man who ran over her with his car was never arrested. The nineteen police officers on trial – who either stood by or actively participated – were released with official warnings. Zain ul-Abedeen, the amulet-seller, later had his death sentence commuted.

Farkhunda's family, who had been brave enough to speak up and pursue a legal battle, fled the country, so real were the threats against them. The investigation, it turned

out, had been perfunctory and patchy, a rushed job concluded in two months. It was more a show to appease the
world's media, who had picked up on the story, than any
real reckoning.

After this, I was not sure exactly what I would do when
I returned to Kabul in 2016, but my mind and heart were
set on one thing: I would take everything I had learnt,
all the skills and resilience I had developed, and fight
with my teeth and elegantly painted nails for women like
Farkhunda.

Four

I feel at my strongest when I am talking with women, hearing their problems and sharing their pain. Although I have no fear of public speaking, and positively enjoy being on stage and addressing a room, I gather my energy through one-to-one interactions.

For decades women have been pushed into the background in Afghanistan, but each one of them has a remarkable story. Usually that story is a tragedy, marked by the deaths of their menfolk. Afghanistan's perma-war has slaughtered swathes of every living generation, and if a woman is not a widow by the time she reaches middle age, she will almost certainly have lost her son, brother or father. I can understand how that feels. I come to these women not as the politician who wins awards and addresses world leaders, but as Zarifa, the Afghan girl whose body and heart is as scarred as theirs. I understand how a life defined by pain can still be marked with moments of joy; how the simple act of surviving as a woman in a place like

Afghanistan, of learning how to read and write, and earning your own money, is a victory more significant than an Olympic gold.

'*Zarifa?*' Afghan women who recognise me on the street often address me by my first name only, as if I were their sister or long-lost school friend. Many of them are slightly shy at first. They see how I argue back with the television interviewers, and think I must be abrupt and rude. Actually, I am, but only with people who deserve it. To women, and especially to those who are suffering, I show my other face – the Zarifa who cries with them when they open their hearts.

I am proudest when I am recognised by a young woman who is forging a path for herself, like the airline stewardess who recognised me as she was collecting my empty food tray on a recent flight I took. For five minutes she stopped work and told me how she had studied English and then used her degree to get this job that was allowing her to see a world outside Afghanistan. I felt a warmth surge through me as I studied her confident face, beautifully made up underneath her loose headscarf, a stylish watch on her wrist that she had bought with her own paycheque. By the time she moved on I felt that we were friends.

The girl seated next to me on that flight was in a different state of mind. For the first twenty minutes after take-off, she rested her head against the seat in front, her eyes scrunched tight. When she turned to me to ask whether I had any painkillers I could see that she had been crying. Hania was twenty-two years old and leaving Afghanistan for the first time in her life to travel to Hungary, to marry a man she only knew through phone calls and photographs.

It was not a forced marriage – she genuinely loved him, and was excited about the new life awaiting her. But at the same time, she was in anguish. She did not know when she would see her family again. In the check-in area at Kabul airport, I had spotted her tearful farewell with her brother.

I am only five years older than Hania, but felt an overwhelming urge to take care of her. An Afghan upbringing had left her entirely unprepared for this moment. Yet I knew that, once she started tasting freedom, she would be happier than she could ever have imagined possible.

'You have to take care of your own life,' I told her. 'You feel bad about leaving your family, but if you die tomorrow in Afghanistan then you are no good to anybody. Go, and enjoy yourself. Today is a bad day for you, but life is long, and it will be filled with many more happy ones.'

Hania and I swapped numbers, and she asked whether I would come to her wedding.

'Of course,' I told her. 'And I want you to keep in touch with me and let me know how you are doing.'

For the next twenty-four hours, we stayed together in the transit lounge, waiting for my connection to Germany and hers to Budapest. Hania spoke to her mother, telling her that she had met a nice Afghan lady on the flight and she was looking after her. She had no idea who I was. But I hope she could see that she had an ally.

When I was Hania's age, I had just returned to Kabul from India and begun setting up my life. It was a rare thing for an unmarried young woman to live on her own in Afghanistan, but after so many years living independently I didn't want to move back in with my family, so I decided to rent a place on my own. I loved my apartment from the moment the estate agent first opened the door. It was on the tenth floor of a new block in the north of the city, its windows facing south to a sweeping view of the snow-topped mountains that glow at night with the lights of shanty towns. Its front room was huge and sparse, with a parquet floor and clean white walls. In the late afternoons the sun streamed through the windows, throwing warm light onto every surface. Its balcony was small but sur-rounded with high walls that turned it into a private space. In the mornings, I would head out there with my huge mug of coffee and my yoga mat, stretching out my body and blocking all my worries from my mind.

I also threw myself straight into work. I had the quali-fications to take up a bureaucratic job in the government, but soon after I started I realised that I needed to be out among the women I was determined to serve. So when one of my colleagues called to ask for my help setting up a women's project, I agreed, and went to meet him at the directorate of information and culture.

I barely noticed the man sitting in the corner of the office. He was dressed head to toe in brown: brown trou-sers, brown waistcoat, brown shoes, as if he was trying to blend into the carpet. His face was kind but not striking, with warm eyes set deep into crinkled sockets and a mouth that turned up at the corners. His hair was thick and still dark, unlike most Afghan men in their thirties, who tend to turn prematurely grey with stress. He didn't say any-thing in the whole hour I was there. Yet this was the man who would become my business partner, my best friend and then my fiancé.

Bashir Mohammadi is one of the very best men in Afghanistan. If you catch us in the middle of one of our rows, you might think that we cannot stand each other. I am the loud one, always quick to raise my voice when we disagree. Underneath his calm exterior Bashir is just as stubborn as I am, and when he believes that he is right it is almost impossible to get him to back down. But I like this about him. You might think that, as a strong woman in a place where every man is a little dictator, I would prefer a partner who always deferred to me. Actually, the opposite is true: I always knew that I needed to find a man who would challenge me, and not simply take up the role stereotypically played by a woman while I acted like the man. Neither did I want a man whose fragile ego might be bruised when he played the supporting role. Bashir and I know that, behind our backs, others gossip but neither of us cares a bit.

We have had so many experiences and so much fun together. We have travelled in India, as I showed him the places I discovered as a student. We have driven all over Kabul and further afield, laughing at the gawping stares we get when I take the wheel and he sits in the passenger seat beside me. On winter evenings in Kabul we would gather all of our friends in my apartment, and together sing old Afghan folk songs at the top of our voices while Bashir accompanied us on his accordion. I had some friends before I met him, but I was mostly going through life alone, usually feeling misunderstood. Now I always have someone beside me, even when he is not physically there. I do not love him because he buys me presents or is there straight away when I need something. I love him because he just gets me, and what I am trying to do. Other people might see me as this difficult, often abrasive woman, working to get glory, or attention, or money. I never had to explain to Bashir that that is not my purpose. He instinctively understands that I am doing what I do because I want Afghanistan, my motherland, to be a better place – and that is what he wants too.

What's more, he sees me as a woman. In order to get to where I have, I have had to cover up parts of my femininity, to the point where I almost forgot my gender. With Bashir, I can shed those layers of armour that I have gathered around myself, knowing that he will not respect me any less when I show him my softer, more sentimental side. When we fled Kabul in August 2021, I reached instinctively for my engagement photos. It may seem like an odd choice for me to have made: why not my degree certificates, or mementos from my work? I chose those photos because they remind me of who I really am, underneath this exterior that I have built for public consumption: a woman who can be just as feminine as any other, and just as capable of being loved.

That first meeting became the source of our first argument. Bashir still insists that he asked me for my phone number that day, when I remember clearly that he did not! He was too shy and instead got his friend to ask me that evening. Either way, once we started talking I was glad that he did. For me, it was very normal: in India I had plenty of male friends, and nobody ever thought it meant anything more. But this was Afghanistan, where everybody is always casting their own aspersions. Moreover, I was twenty-two and still single – something of an anomaly in a country where girls are usually married or at least engaged by the time they turn twenty. As soon as Bashir and I started to get to know each other, everyone was whispering about marriage. But I did not see us like that. We were two people with similar dreams for our country: for it to be peaceful, progressive and fair. We realised early on that we would work well together.

I wanted to set up a radio station. I had considered starting a newspaper or website, but I thought that radio would be the best way for me to reach out to as many women as possible. When I was a child, it was through our radio that my family received most of their information about what was happening in the country. Radio sets are cheap, so even the most impoverished families in Afghanistan have one. With a little equipment and a small team, it would be possible for me to broadcast programmes to a wide area, and women who were stuck at home would be able to tune in and listen. I did not want to do this in Kabul. Though life was far from perfect there, Kabuli women had far more open lives than those in other parts of the country and there were already several radio stations there that served them. They did not need my project in Kabul: I thought Paktia would be the best place. I knew the area well, and understood the problems women there were facing.

Everything had grown exponentially worse in Afghanistan during the years I spent in India. The US began its steady withdrawal of troops in 2011, and by the time they realised what was happening it was too late. The Taliban expanded its reach in sync with the US pullout, the insurgents even managing to briefly take control of Kunduz city, in the province where my mother grew up – the first time they had controlled a regional capital since 2001. Tens of thousands of people were displaced as the national army fought to retake the city. It was just one of many such battles underway across the country. Huge parts of the southern province of Helmand fell to the Taliban in late 2015 and early 2016, with very little fight from the security forces. This was partly due to endemic corruption within the military bureaucracy. Generals often inflated their troop numbers with 'ghost soldiers', who existed only on paper, in order to increase the budget they received from the ministry and cream off money for themselves. By 2016, the US had already poured US$113 billion into reconstruction in Afghanistan, with 60 per cent of that money going to the security forces. Yet almost as quickly as the resources flowed in, so much of it leaked straight back out to the Taliban. Each time the group captured a new area, it also got its hands on the local arsenals, well stocked with US-supplied weapons. And as the situation worsened, US officials were increasingly unable to monitor the reconstruction projects they had funded.

The US was losing its influence, but we were losing our blood. 2015 was the deadliest year on record for Afghan civilians: 3,500 people were killed, a quarter of them children, and 7,500 wounded. The number of women killed or injured in attacks was soaring, up by more than a third from the year before, since the extremists were increasingly waging their war by attacking soft civilian targets. When the Taliban took over Kunduz, they went for the women first, targeting activists and ransacking the offices of women's aid organisations. One previously promising development, the nomination of Anisa Rasouli as Afghanistan's first female supreme court judge, was scuppered thanks to an outcry from conservative members of parliament, who managed to swing the vote against her appointment.

Given what was happening, I knew that it was more important than ever for ordinary women to have a voice in the country. Bashir agreed. But he was not convinced that Paktia was the right place.

'You're from Wardak and that province has lots of problems too!' he told me. 'You should be opening a radio station there.'

He was right, I am technically from Wardak. According to Afghan tradition, your home province is the place where your father's family originate, but I had not been to Wardak since the month I spent with my cousin in the autumn of 2001. I felt I was Kabuli, born and bred: a daughter of the colourful mix of cultures that makes up Afghanistan's capital city. I also remembered, even after all those years, just how conservative Wardak was. I had been able to handle it when I was a child, but knew that as an adult, unbearable expectations would be placed on me there.

Nonetheless, I respected Bashir's opinion. I appreciated the fact that he never tried to talk me out of doing something altogether, like my family often did; his criticisms were only ever constructive. So when he suggested that we take a look at Wardak ourselves, I agreed. Together, we drove to Maidan Shahr, the provincial capital, me wearing a long dress and a headscarf and sitting in the passenger seat beside Bashir. Since I had returned from India I had gone back to wearing the scarf in my old style, draped loosely over my hair rather than tightly around my face. As we left the western limits of Kabul, I began feeling apprehensive. I thought about Qabila, my cousin in Wardak, and how she had dressed like an old aunty even when she was a little girl. I worried too about how active the Taliban had been recently in this region. Along the sole road from Kabul to Maidan Shahr there was a section that was notorious for insurgent attacks. It was a poor, industrial area, scattered with low compounds where workers laid bricks out to dry in the sun. Attackers would suddenly appear from the maze with a gun or a rocket launcher, fire on their target and then melt away, knowing they would be sheltered by sympathetic locals. Sometimes they would plant roadside bombs, triggering them remotely as their victims drove past. The road was one of the most bombed in the country, each blast adding a new crater to its cartography. It was always a bad sign if the workshops were empty; it often meant that the Taliban had warned locals to get out of the way. This time we were lucky. We passed through the danger zone with no problems, and I started to relax. But my good mood was short-lived: I had a new problem to consider. I realised that the few women I could see on the streets on Maidan Shahr were all wearing burkas, triggering hazy memories of the Kabul of my childhood. I doubt they had ever seen a woman in a loose scarf, let alone one sitting next to a man in the passenger seat of a car. Soon, men were staring at us as we drove along. It was an eerie, uncomfortable experience: how I imagine life must be for a member of a royal family or a celebrity, only without the adoration.

Bashir had found a location that would make a perfect base for a radio station. It was in the middle of Maidan Shahr, spacious, and with good security. The rent was reasonable; we would be funding the project ourselves, and needed to watch our costs. There was only one thing that didn't bode well – the building had last been used as a prison. My skin prickled as we walked through the door. Everything had been left as it was the day the prisoners were moved out: names scratched into the walls of what had once been cells, rusty chains attached to hooks in the walls, and dark basement rooms that must have been used for interrogations – the air down there still crackled with vicious energy. In the places where Taliban members had once been locked up, we would hold meetings to work out how we could appeal to the women of the region. In place of the state sign that had once hung over the entrance, we would put up our station logo. It was hardly an auspicious start, but one thing had convinced me that Bashir was right, that Wardak was the place where we should broadcast. I had done my market research and discovered that, although there were already several radio stations operating in this region, not a single one had a female presenter. All of them were too intimidated by the near-presence of the Taliban to even take a question from a female caller. Women had literally been silenced in Wardak.

We called the radio station Peghla, which in Pashto means young girl. Even though I had given way to Bashir on the place we chose, the name was one thing I wouldn't budge on, even though I knew immediately that it would make waves.

'The province isn't going to accept this!' Bashir said, as we prepared the licence paperwork.

Peghla is a loaded word, like many in the Pashto language that are connected to women. It carries the implication that the girl it refers to is a virgin, something close to 'maiden' in English. According to conservatives, even the nod to sex that it confers is shameful.

'Peghla?!' exclaimed Zundi Gun Zamani, the Wardak governor, when I told him about our plans. 'I think a station for women is a great idea, but can't you give it a different name?'

I was ready for the fight; all those years of battling my own family had prepared me well for moments like this.

'No way,' I told him. 'If the radio station is to happen, this is the name it will have.'

The ridiculous thing was, after all the debates and anguish it caused me, the name wasn't even what provoked the most criticism. Before our launch, I had joined a Mother's Day celebration with members of the local council and other officials. It was the perfect opportunity to explain our project and tell them how happy I was that we would be broadcasting from Wardak. Afterwards, the local representative of the Radio and Television Authority came up to me.

'People aren't happy with you,' he said. 'You called the province "Wardak".'

What? I could not believe what I was hearing. This was a grudge that stemmed back decades, and had nothing to do with me. Maidan Shahr had once been part of Kabul, until it was declared the official capital of Wardak by King Mohammed Zahir Shah in the 1960s. The people of Wardak were furious. To them, this was yet another example of distant rulers imposing their will over their province. The petty row has been passed down through generations like an heirloom, and still today proud Wardakis fume when someone stands in Maidan Shahr and declares it part of Wardak, as I had just done in the meeting. They insist that another town should be chosen as the regional capital, although wild and empty Wardak is hardly full of big towns. The people of Maidan Shahr have an equal disdain for the Wardak villagers, feeling themselves far too sophisticated to be lumped together with them. They are adamant that the province should be called Maidan Wardak, to let everyone know that their refined urbanity has been thrown into the mix.

I could not even be bothered arguing over it – I left it for the etymological purists to sort out. In late 2016, after we had scrubbed out the old prison, removed the chains and painted the walls, and set up a studio and offices in the old cell blocks, I became the first female voice on the Wardak airwaves.

'Hello, everyone,' I said in our inaugural broadcast. 'This is Peghla radio. We're focused on women's rights, and we're here to try to tell you the facts.'

Our first months were beset with unforeseen problems, although in hindsight they seemed obvious. My main concern before we launched had been logistics: both Bashir and I continued to live separately in Kabul, commuting to Maidan Shahr each day. It was a short distance but still a tiring and dangerous drive. I worried every day that we might be attacked on the road, which ran through some of the most restive Taliban territory. But our problems were more pedestrian. First was funding. We had launched on a shoestring, by using equipment Bashir already owned and employing a small team. We hoped we would soon be able to get money flowing in through advertising. But no local businesses would buy slots, even after several months, and we were still using our own money to keep the station going. Part of the problem was that there was no real culture of business advertisement on radio stations in Wardak. The bigger issue, though, was that with our single antenna set up in the city centre, our signal couldn't penetrate the mountainous terrain to reach the villages nestled in the valleys – the very places we wanted to reach, where the Taliban's grip was strongest. To get our programmes heard there, we needed a second antenna on top of the tallest mountain in the area. That was Dasht-e-Top, a ridge of bald peaks looking over the plain below. Once a weekend destination for Kabulis looking to escape the oppressive heat and pollution of the city, it was filled with holiday chalets set among its meadow grasses and streams. That era was deep in the past, however. The badlands around Dasht-e-Top were now the Taliban's main local strongholds.

There was a police academy at Dasht-e-Top, a tough outpost that came under constant attack from the militants. Once, sometimes twice a week, Taliban fighters would sneak through the mountain paths and start firing on the guards. On other evenings, officers would watch helplessly as Taliban columns passed across the flatlands on their way to operations in neighbouring Logar province. In order to take them on in a firefight, the police chief at Dasht-e-Top needed permission from his superiors in Kabul, so unless the Taliban fired first, the officers would simply watch as they marched across the landscape and melted into local villages. Although the police officers were surprised when I pulled up at their gate alone in my car one bright, chilly afternoon, I was hardly the worst visitor they could have had. I explained my plan to the chief, who agreed to send me out with one of his men so that I could place the antenna in the highest point I could find.

Once that was up and running, Peghla FM boomed. Our signal could be heard all over the province, and we began assembling a proper schedule with music programmes and chat shows. With this, came revenue. Some of our team started going out and selling advertising slots at the bargain rate of 50 Afghani a minute. As well as the adverts, between every show we played an ident of my voice reminding listeners what the station was about.

I didn't just want to talk to people with my radio station: I wanted to listen to them. We travelled all around the city with our small recorder, chatting to locals about the things that bothered them. The Taliban was an issue for many, sure, but we found that other things – the terrible state of the roads, the lack of good schools and the rising prices of basic goods in the shops – were of equal importance. I visited the only girls' school in the city, a tiny building set within a huge compound, its roof broken and the air stifling. The girls sat cross-legged on the ground. They weren't having to hold their breath every time they heard footsteps, but otherwise, nothing much had changed since I had been at school during the Taliban era. I went to hospitals and maternity wards, interviewing female doctors and patients and broadcasting their stories. I hoped it would help the women listening out in the countryside realise that there were facilities available to them when they were sick or giving birth, and that they didn't have to endure these things at home. Meanwhile, as our audience grew, calls to our programmes started flooding in. The women who wanted to speak to us rarely gave their names – that would have been far too dangerous. They called when the men in their families were out of the house, and listened to our shows secretly as they cleaned and cooked. I thought I was aware of all that was happening in my country, but what they told us was shocking. There were girls saying they were desperate to go to school, but that their fathers would not allow it, or that there were no schools for girls in their area. There were others, young teenagers, who wept as they described how they were being forced into marriages with older men. Many of the older women described how they were beaten by their husbands for the slightest thing, be it not cleaning the house to his liking or daring to answer back.

There was one girl in particular who called often. Like the others, she would never give her name. 'Just call me a lover of this radio station,' she would say. But every time she was put through, I knew who it was by her soft voice. She would come on air and say how much she loved listening to our programmes, how they were teaching her more about the world. She said she wanted to be an educated woman and to work to make Afghanistan a better place. Sometimes she recited poems on air in her fluent, melodic tones. But she also described how her father had decided that she should get married, that there was nothing she could do to stop it. She had never met the man chosen for her. I didn't know how to respond. If I said it was a bad thing, what would it have changed for her? She knew as much already: it would only hurt her and make her more despondent. Sometimes I wondered what would happen if I found out her identity, and where she lived, if I could go to her house and try to talk her family out of it. There was only one way that could end. 'Who are you to interfere in our family affairs?' they would say, and there would be nothing more that I could do. A girl in Afghanistan could be married at fifteen if her father approved. The law banning forced marriage was rarely implemented, particularly in areas where the Taliban was stronger than the state. The only thing such an intervention would achieve would be more problems for the girl, who would be punished for talking about private matters with a stranger. One day, inevitably, she stopped calling. I never did find out what became of her.

Once the radio station was well established and my name was known around Maidan Shahr, I decided that the time was right to start using my profile more assertively, to prove that empowering women meant empowering everyone. A group of young men from Helmand province, the Taliban's southern heartlands, had set off on a peace march to Kabul, a 450-mile journey through lawless territory that would take them nearly six weeks. They had been spurred into action by a brutal Taliban car bombing at a football match in Laskhar Gah, which killed dozens of innocent people. Their demands were simple, and hardly excessive:

they wanted a ceasefire, and the start of political dialogue between all Afghan parties. When I heard what they were doing, my heart jumped: this was the kind of non-violent, attention-grabbing action that Afghanistan needed. For decades, our first resort had always been the gun, but there was a new generation that was sick of the killing. Now, finally, they were raising their voices, rather than weapons.

Wardak would be the last province the marchers passed through before they entered Kabul, and I decided to organise a huge demonstration to greet them. It would be a gesture of solidarity that would motivate them for the final leg, and a powerful message to the Taliban that women, too, were brave enough to stand up to them. In April 2018, the column of men, footsore but smiling, entered the area. I had organised a drummer, and roused young men from the city, and I stood at the head of our parade with my megaphone – the sole woman in a crowd of men, walking down roads that cut through Taliban villages.

'Drop the weapon and take a pen!' I shouted. 'We want peace! We want education!'

I knew that many of the men walking behind me would, until that day, have choked at the idea that they would be led by a woman. But even if they would have preferred to be following a man at that protest, when they were presented with a woman they accepted. I hoped that every one of them might go back to their families and look at their wives, sisters and mothers in a new way, and from now on see them as people who could also lead a protest. From that one action, the lives of several hundred women might potentially change for the better.

Inside, I felt ecstatic. Ever since I spoke to Hamid Karzai

aged nine, I have been thrilled by public speaking, and have always loved hearing my voice amplified through a loudspeaker. I will admit that I am one of those people who loves the limelight, so long as it is on my terms. I may have felt shy when a roomful of eyes were on me at my engagement party, but when I was the centre of attention at that protest, I revelled in it. Whether the feeling of the crowd towards me was good or bad, I didn't care: I just loved that their eyes and thoughts were fixed on me, giving me a platform, and a voice.

Our team and listeners were growing. We had taken on several staff, young Wardakis who understood what we were trying to achieve. There was Sifat, a fit young guy who was studying to be a teacher and, apart from doing the evening shows on the radio, spent all his free time exercising. He later got a job at Kandahar University, and despite the fact that his family expected to arrange his marriage, he fell in love with a woman he met and battled everyone to marry her. I was crushed when I heard later that he had died in a car crash on his way home from the university. It seemed so wrong that someone who was trying to change his life should lose it; to this day I still pray for him.

Sifat presented his show alongside Ihsan, the pair of them developing an easy back-and-forth routine in which they discussed everything from politics to the daily annoyances of life in Afghanistan. Ihsan was a very clever guy but hid it well – he was constantly making us laugh by acting the fool. I was disappointed that I couldn't take on a female team at the station, but I knew that would be the case when I decided to set it up outside Kabul. The notion that any men in Wardak would allow their daughters or wives to broadcast their voices into the homes of strangers was impossible. But at least I knew that women were listening.

It didn't take long for the Taliban to tune in to Peghla FM, too. Usually I commuted to Maidan Shahr each day, since the city was a dangerous place at night. The journey took about an hour each way, depending on how terrible the traffic was. Sometimes I would drive back with Bashir, otherwise I would take a shared taxi. But one particular night, I had worked too late to return to my home in Kabul, so I rolled out a sleeping mat in one of the offices and asked Habib, the caretaker we employed, to bring me some food from the market. Two minutes later he was knocking at the door, and I opened it to find him ashenfaced and shaking.

'Miss Ghafari,' he said. 'Someone has pinned a letter to the gate.'

Habib, a sweet and kind man of about thirty, scared easily; he started at every noise outside the office at night. I never took him too seriously, but this time he was clearly shaken up.

'It'll be nothing,' I reassured him. 'Come on, let's go and take a look.'

The street was pitch black and appeared to be deserted. The letter, a piece of paper, flapping gently in the breeze, had the seal of the Taliban at its top: a black-and-white image of the Quran, surrounded by curling ears of corn and underneath, in Arabic: 'There is no god but Allah.'

I snatched it off the gate, and began reading. The letter was addressed to me. It read:

Zarifa Ghafari. You started this radio station to distract our women from their right path. You are teaching them bad things, against our religion and traditions. If you don't stop these activities, anything that happens to you or the radio station will be your responsibility.

I nearly laughed. What clichés! It was as if they had been inspired by B-list gangster films. It took me a few seconds to get over the hilarity and realise the danger we were in. Habib and I hurried back inside, and I called the district police chief and governor. The next morning, they sent officers over to take an official record of the incident, and warned me to be careful.

How? I wondered. *What exactly should I do?*

I knew that many in Wardak were angry about the station, and were particularly affronted by me, a woman with a habit of speaking her mind. Even those men who weren't extremists generally couldn't handle an opinion-ated woman. One evening, when I had taken a shared taxi from Maidan Shahr to Kabul, I listened with increasing exasperation at the conversation unfolding between the three men in the car. One of them said his son was working as a labourer in Britain, and wanted his pregnant wife to join him. Both he and the others huffed as they concurred that it was a terrible idea.

'Nobody prays there!' the father said. 'There are no Muslims in England!'

I couldn't keep silent. 'I'm also a passenger in this car, so I'm going to share my thoughts.'

The men fell silent, like in saloon bars in Westerns when a stranger walks in.

'Who are you to stop a wife from joining her husband? And who exactly has told you this lie that there are no Muslims in England?'

They immediately rounded on me.

'This is a matter of religion! How can you know anything about these things?'

All I could do was roll my eyes. They were so used to assuming they were right that the suggestion they might be wrong was a joke to them – especially when it came from a woman. These kind of patronising putdowns are something that all Afghan women have to learn to bear. But even as I laughed such insults off, I was always wondering – were these men capable of doing me real harm?

Practically, there was little we could do to protect ourselves from the Taliban. We had already installed security systems, and were alert to the people gathering around us when we went into the city to record our news reports. I was determined that we would not stop broadcasting. Still, after the threat we were all a little more nervous. A few months later, when Habib came to me again and said he had spotted a strange package propped up against the wall, I took him seriously. We went outside to take a look. The package was wrapped in white cotton and string, about the size of a shoebox. The Taliban had become expert bombmakers, rigging even tiny devices with powerful explosives and shards of sharp metal that tore through the flesh of anyone nearby. These days, they had also learned how to detonate them with mobile phone signals, meaning that this package might explode at any moment. We rushed back inside and I called the police chief again.

Within minutes, he was at our office with his men. Soon, the whole area filled with police and soldiers erecting road-blocks and directing people away from the area. They told us to stand back while they turned on a signal jammer, and then one of them approached the package with a stick. We all watched intently, holding our breath, as he started to poke at it gently, expertly teasing open the tie at the top. In the moment the fabric fell open we gasped – and then started laughing uncontrollably. Inside were two battered old Qurans that someone had left out for the scrap collectors. They had wrapped them up to save them the indignity of touching the ground. All this fuss, and the centre of Maidan Shahr brought to a standstill.

For the first few months that Bashir and I worked together, I kept our relationship purely business. I was hard on him: I wanted to exert my authority over the project. I never joked with him, or spent time in idle chat. I let him know that any decisions had to go through me. Looking back, maybe I was testing him. I needed him to know that I was never going to be the typical Afghan woman, deferring to him and doing everything I could to make him feel like the powerful man. If he was serious about wanting to marry me, then he had to accept me as his equal, and not just initially, but for ever. After we had dealt with several crises together at the radio station, I started to see that he was sincere. He had never once talked over me, nor discounted my opinion as most men tend to do. He had been entirely comfortable letting me take the starring role in our programmes. And it was clear that he cared about women's rights as much as I did. Bashir was an unusual Afghan man indeed.

After two years we relaxed into a comfortable friendship. Bashir told me he was unhappy with his life, even though he had plenty of friends and a good job outside the radio station at the directorate of culture. But he did not want to marry just any woman. He wanted someone with a good education and her own ideas. I knew he was really talking about me.

One evening we stayed up late at the radio station, talking about our lives, our dreams and our deepest thoughts. It was my final test for him. I wanted him to know everything about me, so that he could really be aware of who I was and what I wanted from my life. When he later drove me home and dropped me off, I sat up for hours, my mind spinning. He respected me. He showed me his love. Could I give him the happiness he wanted so much, and which he deserved? What was stopping me? *If I am the one who can give him that happiness then why not*, I thought.

It wasn't the romantic way to do it, but I didn't want to keep him waiting any longer, and sent him a text:

'If you want to marry me,' I wrote, 'I accept.'

Seconds later, his reply flashed onto my screen.

There are many stages to getting married in Afghanistan. First comes the proposal and acceptance. But you are not considered officially engaged until you have thrown a huge party. It is as big, sometimes bigger, than your actual wedding ceremony, and just as important. Before you even get engaged, however, you have to go through a rather dated performance.

Bashir's extended family and mine sat in my own family's home, the men in one room and the women in another, surrounded by baskets full of sweets and flowers. I had known Bashir for so long already that the rituals around our engagement felt strange. In this part of the ritual, the woman is expected to be quiet and shy, gazing at the floor and giggling behind her hand. I am not that kind of woman. If anything, I felt it would be embarrassing to act that way. When I was eventually led into the room where the women were sitting, playing music and dancing together, I was nevertheless required to sit demurely in the corner. My mother even stopped me from clapping, telling me that it didn't look good and that people might gossip. Even the most open-minded Afghans are penned in by the pressure of traditions.

The other thing that I was expected to do was cry. It is meant to be such a sad occasion, leaving home, even though you are starting a family of your own. If you don't cry, people might wonder why you seem to be so happy. For me, this was ridiculous. I already lived on my own! And my family didn't need to see my tears to know that I loved them. Finally, when all this role-playing was over and I was back in my own apartment, Bashir and I snuck off together and drove around the city. This, to me, was the real celebration, with no other eyes on us and no expectations to meet. He didn't stop smiling all night.

We held our official engagement in one of Kabul's wedding halls in front of three hundred friends and family – a small number by Afghan standards. I think I was the first woman in Kabul to wear only one dress throughout.

Usually it is a fashion show, with an outfit change every couple of hours. But once I tried on the pink dress with red flowers, I knew that was all I needed. I was never much of a girly-girl — we didn't have the money for lots of clothes when I was a child, and by the time I was an adult there were other things more important to me. But that day I spent hours getting my hair and make-up done. When I looked in the mirror I hardly recognised myself: my skin was flawless and my eyes looked wide and bright. I didn't care what anyone thought of me that night. I danced with Bashir and he kissed my forehead in front of everyone, and I ate the food, too, which the bride usually does not. I hardly wore any jewellery, another thing for people to gossip about, since the bride is usually decked out in the gold the groom's family has given to her as a dowry. To me, these traditions symbolised women's inferior place in society, making her into a mute thing — a chattel — that could be bought by a man. I wanted to tear up these traditions, do it my way and not give a damn.

At the end of the night, with my feet aching in the high heels I had been dancing in all evening, we posed for our official photographs, grinning widely with happiness. When I compare my engagement photos to others I have seen, in which the couples look bewildered and scared, I always feel so proud. Bashir and I looked like a couple that you might see anywhere else in the world. I was sure that everything could only get better from here.

A combination of bad luck and unexpected events never allowed us to get that far. We celebrated our engagement in March 2020 with a small party in one of Kabul's new wedding halls, and had planned to hold our wedding in November that year. When tragedy overtook us, we pushed the date back to September 2021. But by then, we had fled our country. My dress was already chosen. It was beautiful, even more so than my engagement dress: a simple sleeveless white gown that my aunt had brought from Germany, embroidered on the front and with a small fishtail train at the back. My father had planned to surprise me with it on the day he died. For months, the dress hung in my wardrobe, untouched. I have never even tried it on.

Five

There is a certain type of hoodlum in Kabul who is immediately recognisable by his outfit, an odd mix of styles: a baggy long shirt with buttons down the front and huge puffy sleeves; trousers cut short to show off his ankles and knock-off trainers; a chequered Arab-style scarf around his neck; and his hair gelled into a quiff like one of the chiselled male models in the barbershop windows – an ideal of beauty he aspires to, though our subject is usually undernourished. He calls himself a *Bacha-e Kaaka*, a *Rayees* or a *Shah*, basically the boss of the neighbourhood, and hangs around with others who are dressed like him. They smoke, drink alcohol and harass women, think they own the city streets and walk with an exaggerated swagger to show it. They thrive on violence, and confuse fear with respect. Nobody dares challenge them when they spit on the pavement or steal from a street vendor. Although they care little for the edicts of Islam, they are always quick to join in when a woman is being persecuted on religious grounds. It was the *Bacha-e Kakaa* who often jeered at my sisters and me as we walked around Kabul in jeans. The mob that lynched Farkhunda Malikzada included a heavy contingent of *Bacha-e Kaaka*, too.

These marauding gangs did not exist when the Taliban controlled the country; they are a result of the freedoms that came after 2001. With the extremists gone the streets returned to normal Afghans, but not everyone knew how to use them. Gang members do not tend to come from the original Kabul families, but from those who emigrated to the capital from the countryside during the long, violent years of the civil war. They are often still made to feel like outsiders, even if they are the third generation to be born there. Usually uneducated and illiterate, they drift towards crime rather than low-paid work in a city where jobs are scarce. Without a decent wage, they are unable to buy or even rent a house, a necessity for a man if he wants to marry. In a conservative place like Afghanistan, it is rare that an unmarried man can find a girlfriend, or even have a platonic friendship with a woman who is not his blood relative. And so the *Bacha-e Kaaka* remain poor, alienated and frustrated, taking it out on everyone around them.

Kabul is a city of light and dark, of *Bacha-e Kaaka* weaving through the alleyways alongside bearded mullahs and tutting old grandmas. It is an ancient city scarred by its traumatic modernity, its layers as visible as in slices of sedimentary rock. By the time I returned from India it was a dangerous city, too, but these tensions gave it its energy, a buzzing vitality that I always found to be a remedy for my own mental exhaustion. Whenever I felt dragged down by life, I would climb behind the wheel of a car and turn the music on the stereo up loud, swerving around the potholes as I drove through the city with my window down. Every time, something new would catch my eye in this place that I have known all my life.

On the highway through the old city, as it crossed the river, I would see ghostly figures ducking out from the litter-strewn bank under the Pol-e Sohkta bridge. These were the victims of the poppies that light up swathes of Afghanistan in glorious purples and whites in the springtime, a gorgeous flash before the petals wither and the poppy's sap, its addictive poison, seeps out. The Taliban, despite its public proclamations against the drug, tolerated and encouraged the industry as a source of revenue in the 1990s. After the Taliban fell, opium production soared; four-fifths of the world's heroin starts life in Afghanistan's poppy fields. Most of the product is destined for the streets of Western Europe, but enough stays in Afghanistan to shatter lives there, too. In 2005 there were around 200,000 Afghan opium addicts. A decade later, there were nearly 3 million, spilling out onto the streets of every town and city.

These drug problems drove a tsunami of petty crime that crashed over the country. Like most Muslim cities, Kabul used to be a place largely unafflicted by street robberies, such is the shame of stealing in Islam. But after 2001, you always had to be on your guard. When I met up with groups of friends for coffee, our conversation would often turn to the latest scams. I heard of unscrupulous taxi drivers taking part in set-ups in which they drew your attention away with endless small talk while another passenger rifled through your pockets, and skilled urchins who would lift wallets out of bags with astounding dexterity as they bumped into their victims on the pavements. As the years passed, I started hearing more anecdotes about knife and gunpoint holdups in the city centre, with some attackers even bold enough to hijack cars on the highways. The most organised street criminals nurtured their connections inside the police force, who were given generous back-handers to look the other way.

It is easy to level the blame at these boys, and mark their crimes and attitudes down to failures of character and upbringing. But there are other deep-rooted reasons, entwined with the corrosion of Afghan society. The *Bacha-e Kaaka* and the opium addicts are at the bottom of a tower of criminality that looms over the country, casting its shadow on everything. The warlords' men were the original hoodlums; though they were subdued and pushed to the margins by the Taliban, they never quite gave up. Instead, they shrank away to regions north of the capital, the villages of the Panjshir valley and Shamali plain, where they bided their time. After 2001, as the Taliban was ousted and Kabul became a more dangerous place to live and work, the warlords made themselves indispensable by offering their 'protection services' to business owners and high-profile people, including politicians. Others realised that there was money to be made from extortion: newly arrived foreign diplomats and aid workers became easy targets for kidnapping rings. Some of the best-known gang leaders and warlords wrangled positions within the new government and security forces, and worked the system to their own benefit – often juggling both roles at once.

The cleverest criminals got into land-grabbing, a practice that began with the mujahideen, who took whatever they wanted at the barrel of a gun. That included property – if the militiamen liked the look of a house or parcel of land, they would find the owner and deliver the bad news. Few were foolhardy enough to object. The warlord-gangs marked up Kabul territory among themselves – a confederacy of criminal jurisdictions.

As I drove out of the choked narrow streets of the old city and crossed the river into the Kabul of wide avenues and brand new buildings, I would enter the warlords' domains. In the shadow of the diplomatic quarter with its storey-high blast walls, there were the smoothly paved streets of Sherpur. This used to be a slum district of mud houses until 2003, when the rising nouveau riche took a liking to the location and sent the bulldozers in. In its place the constructors erected tacky mansions in gaudy colours, arranged behind high walls along wide boulevards. These blank-windowed monstrosities were often four storeys high, with a garage big enough for multiple cars, their grand entrances featuring atrium-style circular foyers rising to moulded plasterwork ceilings, mezzanines at each level that led to en-suite bedrooms. The kitchens were state of the art. These 'poppy palaces' were built by the drug lords and government officials who had seized the land; twenty-nine of them, including six cabinet ministers, were named in reports as having acquired plots in Sherpur. The irony is that many of these mansions have lain empty – there simply isn't much demand for such ostentation in Kabul. Whenever I passed through Sherpur it was a ghost town, its streets devoid of people, its air empty of sound.

In other stolen areas, sprawling, unplanned neighbourhoods cling to the edge of the city. By the time anyone realises that the land they are built on is illegal, the houses have been completed and sold on, with blameless, usually poor people living in them. The government has no cost-effective way of kicking the owners out, so instead they are charged a token fee to retrospectively register the property. That is how Kabul has grown in recent decades, with haphazard tentacles spreading from the centre. And that is how it continues to grow, hopping over the old city walls and expanding up the mountainsides – an unstoppable slow pour of concrete.

From the centre and Sherpur I would drive out westwards, past the shining luxury towers of Shahr-e Naw and onto the long Kampani road, named after the neighbourhood it cuts through. The buildings grew gradually grubbier as I got further from downtown, the tarmac bumpier under my wheels. At Kampani's centre is the Chardihi Market, humming with the call of stallholders and bartering shoppers, its main business taking place behind the scenes, where hitmen-for-hire lurk in smoky tea shops. Chardihi Market was the domain of Zulmai Tufan, a notorious Pashtun warlord. Tufan left his business studies degree at Kabul University to join the Afghan jihad in the 1980s, and by time the civil war burst into Kabul he had 2,000 men on his payroll and several suburbs in the south of the city under his control. He has been accused of committing a massacre in the town of Ashraf in 1993, killing his prisoners by suffocating them with tank chains. In the post-Taliban period he was one of twenty former mujahideen commanders who were offered money under a

UN programme to disarm his militia; he took the proceeds and used them to build up his fiefdom in Kampani. His former acolytes were now the area's organised criminals.

Looping back past a string of new private universities that have sprung up over the past two decades, I would enter the residential suburbs of northern Kabul, where my airy apartment was situated. My peaceful balcony looked out over an area controlled by Hajji Muhammed Almas Zahed, a Tajik warlord who served an apprenticeship under Hekmatyar before defecting to join Ahmad Shah Masood. In the nineties, when the mujahideen controlled Kabul, Zahed was made commander of the army's fifth corps, becoming my father's ultimate boss. He was accused of human rights abuses including killing civilians during the civil war, and later of cooperating with the Taliban in its insurgency against foreign forces, allegations he has denied. After 2001 he became very rich, running businesses including a restaurant, construction projects and a raisin export company; he was also, at the same time, a member of parliament and an advisor to President Ghani.

Continuing clockwise as I cooled off in the air-conditioning and music raised my spirits, I would drive on into eastern Kabul, and the older residential neighbourhoods around the airport. I was slipping across an unseen gang-line now, into the territory of Allah Gul Mujahid, a Hekmatyar protégé who had the nous to slip into politics after 2001, despite having trouble reading and writing. Meanwhile, he was also making his fortune importing goods from China, and spent much of it on building new religious schools I counted as I drove through his neighbourhoods.

Finally I would head south again, back towards the river and the old city, and into the districts controlled by Mullah Tarakhel Mohammadi, a scowling preacher the locals nicknamed 'Crazy Tarakhel'. He too won a place in parliament, though his opponents say he did so by stuffing ballot boxes. Tarakhel denied this, but said that he did urge his tribe to vote for Karzai. In August 2018, when he was banned from standing in elections, he threatened that his supporters would cause havoc. Tarakhel's realms abutted those of Allah Gul Mujahid, and so I tried to avoid the Pul-e Charki road, the dividing line, where there were often shootouts between their militias. Each claimed to command an army of five hundred men; the police rarely intervened to stop the killing.

In one hour's drive, I would pass through each of these places where the crime that had taken over my country stared me in the face; corruption, greed and violence stretching back decades. If I had got in my car feeling defeated, this alone would reignite my determination to create something better for my people, to bring out the lighter, more beautiful sides of Afghanistan's personality.

In March 2018, as Peghla was approaching its second anniversary, I got my first chance to make a real difference: the central government announced that it was holding examinations to appoint mayors to eleven provinces, including Wardak. Mayors did not win their positions by popular vote; instead they were selected by the central government on the basis of their performance in tests. Bashir insisted that I apply. On the one hand, the idea made sense. I was from Wardak, I had a master's degree in economics and, by now, thanks to my work at the radio station, I knew the region and its problems well. I had ambitions to work in public service, and I have always loved a challenge. But a challenge like Wardak? Although I was desperate to help the people of this region, especially its women, I knew how entrenched the problems were. Even the issue of the name, and the rivalry between the people of Maidan Shahr and the villages, would be a hurdle. I had seen for myself how conservative Wardak was, and how powerful the Taliban were here. I knew they would not allow a woman to walk into the job.

Bashir was furious when I said I would not apply. We did not speak for two days. By then we had known each other for two years and our relationship had strengthened into a tight union against the prejudices and limitations of our society. We decided on everything together; apart from my immediate blood family, Bashir was the only person on earth I fully trusted. But this time, he felt a distance between us. No matter how many times I tried to explain my point of view to him, he wouldn't accept it. In the end I relented.

If it's this important to the people close to me, I thought, *it should be important to me, too.*

In Wardak, the land mafias operated differently to those in Kabul. Instead of building on the land they had stolen they often just left it empty, like poker chips they couldn't be bothered to cash in. In Maidan Shahr, one member of parliament had acquired more than three hundred parcels. Another local politician was said to have paid for their land not with money to the municipality, which had owned it, but with bribes to mayors, governors and other city officials. Warlords, Taliban members, politicians, crime bosses – they all participated in the same scheme. Kabul-style overdevelopment is a problem, but so too is Wardak-style underdevelopment. There are gaping spaces in the middle of Maidan Shahr where schools, hospitals or well-planned housing developments could have been built. It still looked more like a village than a proper city, let alone a provincial capital.

I peeled back these layers of corruption and criminality, and the links between the two, as I went out onto the streets of Maidan Shahr with my radio equipment. Maybe it was because I was a woman, or because I had nothing to do with the state, but the decent people of the city opened up to me. They were sick of being forced into this dirty game. Whether you were a businessman wanting to expand your premises or an everyday citizen hoping to get treated at the hospital, you had to pay a bribe if you wanted anything done. This pyramid scheme entangled everyone, yet benefited only those at the top. The rest of us just learned to factor in the extra percentage we had to pay to make sure our documents were processed or our treatments administered. I also discovered what was happening inside the municipality offices: much of the revenue that should have been going into the local budget was instead going to the Taliban, who had supporters inside the council offices. It infiltrated every level – even an influential individual among Maidan Shahr's market traders was in on it. He had set up a system whereby half of the traders' 3,000 Afghani a month business rates went to the Taliban, who in return provided them with a kind of protection from the municipality officials, who would never dare extort a bribe from someone who was paying off the extremists.

While all this money was being sucked out of the state and into the pockets of greedy, violent men, cities like Maidan Shahr remained stuck in time. In the five years before I set up the radio station there had been no development projects in Wardak, save for a five-star hotel. Only a few buildings rose higher than one storey. Most of the roads remained unpaved, just as they had been when my family fled the US bombings for Wardak in 2001. In fact, there were only a handful of proper roads in the region, the highways running from Maidan Shahr to neighbouring provinces Ghazni and Bamyan, and to Kandahar city. The rest of the streets were unpaved, hard and dusty in the dry months, thick with mud during the winter rains and always litter-strewn. When municipal workers cleaned the streets, they took the rubbish half a mile outside the city to an informal dump – a Sisyphean task.

While there were dozens of empty spaces in the middle of the city, new developments were sprawling, unplanned, on the outskirts. Mainly apartment blocks, they were mostly built without proper earthquake precautions, even though Afghanistan lies on fault lines. Most people still burned coal in the winter, its thick smoke mixing with acrid fumes of burning rubbish and car tyres, creating a smog so bad it sometimes blocked out the sun. The sewage system urgently needed updating, and many people relied on septic tanks, which were often poorly maintained and leaked their toxic contents into the earth. There were hardly any green spaces, nothing to make people feel proud. There wasn't just something rotten in the state of Wardak: it was decayed right through to its core.

*

To be eligible for the exams I had to submit a plan of how I would run the municipality, including everything from fighting corruption to developing green areas. I had seen how terribly Wardak was currently being run, so I had the full picture of what I was up against. But thanks to my years in India, I also had a clear idea of how a city should be governed. I decided to base my plan on Chandigarh.

Afghan municipalities are self-funding organisms. They do not take any of their budget from central government but instead through tax revenue collected from local businesses, and from services they provide. These taxes need to be collected properly, and spent on improving the city rather than filling the pockets of corrupt officials and the Taliban. When people can see where their money is being spent, and have some say over what services should be prioritised, they are less likely to avoid paying their taxes. There were other obvious ways to make money, but none had even been considered by Wardak's incumbent administration.

My head was bursting with ideas as I mulled over my application. Although I had initially been reluctant to apply, now that I had, there was little else I could think of. The promise of a new challenge has always galvanised me, and this was no different. Before I started Peghla FM, people in my family had told me that it would not be possible to set up a women's radio station in a place like Wardak. Well, I had proved them wrong on that, and the hit of adrenaline that it had given me was addictive. If I could make the radio station work, then why couldn't I be mayor, too? I started picturing myself in the role as I walked through the streets of Maidan Shahr, how I would speak to the people to convince them that I was there to serve them, not myself.

I have always enjoyed having a platform and power; I can't deny that it gives me a huge sense of personal satisfaction. Taking charge of a situation, one that is going terribly, and steering it towards success is something that thrills me. And although corrupt, inefficient Wardak might have seemed an unappealing prospect, through the lens of my mounting excitement I could see only opportunities.

The province's position as the western gateway to Kabul means that anyone travelling to the capital from Kandahar, Afghanistan's second biggest city, has to pass through it. If there were billboards along that highway, millions of people would see them each year and businesses would queue to buy advertising slots. There was no organised public transport system – it was left to private taxis to offer shared lifts – so establishing a minibus route could bring in revenue and serve the people. If building regulations were properly enforced, the council could establish an engineering and surveying department, which could charge a fee for any application. And if we were to build a proper waste and recycling facility, the rubbish could be converted into fertiliser, energy and paper and, with the money collected, we could begin to improve the environment, in part by the simple act of planting trees and shrubbery.

The most important thing I had learnt in Chandigarh was this: cities have to be governed from the bottom up. It is no use imposing new rules from behind the walls of City Hall and expecting the people to follow them. Citizens must feel a sense of ownership over where they live, which in turn will make them want to keep it as clean and orderly as they keep their own houses. And for that to happen, every single employee of the municipality must be dedicated to working not for themselves, or their tribe, or the Taliban, but for all of the people who live in the city.

When it was announced that I had got through to the next stage of the selection process, Bashir and I ran and jumped around the office in ecstasy, laughing until our faces ached. Our team at the radio station were thrilled too; all our staff at the station were already calling me 'Lady Mayor' as a joke.

I knew that others would be less thrilled. A smear campaign was organised against me on social media, with men posting and reposting the same slew of comments: that I was an immoral woman, or a prostitute. It did not come as a huge surprise. Whenever these kinds of men cannot defeat a woman or feel inferior they turn to gossip. But along with Bashir, I now had another important male ally. My father was mellowing, after all those years when we had so often fought over my choices. I certainly wouldn't say that he had been struck by a feminist epiphany, but he had realised I was stronger and more capable, and certainly more stubborn, than he ever thought I could be. Maybe he was just too old to care about other people's gossip. After I came back from India and began working, I found that his attitude had turned from begrudging acceptance to quiet support. And when I told him that I was planning to apply to become the mayor of Wardak, he encouraged me.

'I can't say I fully support this,' he told me, 'but I don't oppose it. You're going to have hard times with this decision, but don't let that put you off.'

The next stage of the application process – the written exam – would be based on questions about my proposal, to ensure that I had written it myself. When I entered the exam room, I met the competition. One was Mansoor Amiri, the brother of a previous mayor. The third candidate was a former Taliban commander who had managed to sidestep his way into the new government, and was working with the ministry of education. The fourth was a member of Hekmatyar's party, who was also working with the government. It was a true cross-section of Afghan politics. I was the only woman.

We had forty-five minutes to answer four questions. After years of studying in English while I was in India, it had been a long time since I had written anything in Dari or Pashto. But I knew my subject backwards and forwards. As soon as the clock started ticking, I began writing furiously, and soon asked for extra sheets of paper. I was the first to finish, and walked out of the room in my high heels in front of the staring men, my head high under my loose white scarf.

'Let's see how you do,' one of them said, sarcastically, when he emerged.

I did not worry even for a second. I had that pleasant calm feeling in my gut that told me I had done well, and was not surprised when I received the call to tell me I had been shortlisted for the next stage – the interview.

It was held a few days later. I talked to the interviewers for nearly an hour, going into even more detail about my plans to regenerate Wardak. When I came out, Bashir was waiting for me and I was smiling.

'Good news,' I told him. 'I made it.'

Winning the job was only the start of the battle: it would take me another nine months to take up my office in

Wardak. The official confirmation that I had got the job hadn't even been issued before the protests against me began there. As soon as news spread on social media that a woman was in the running for the post, a few men began gathering and shouting slogans against me outside the governor's office in Maidan Shahr. Of all the candidates, I had won top marks in the test and interview, and now it was down to President Ghani to sign the decree. This is when the social media gossip really soured. Some of my opponents said I had paid a bribe to get my high marks – a ridiculous accusation, since I barely had any money. Others said I was a friend of Bibi Gul, the first lady – I wasn't – or that I had used sex to get this far. A classic! All over the world, women who rise up through the ranks are accused of the same.

At the same time I was also overwhelmed with messages of support from all over Afghanistan, and even abroad. Women were thrilled. Many men were, too. But in Maidan Shahr the protests grew. That day, dozens of people gathered in front of the governor's office, some of them shouting that I wasn't even from the city but from Wardak – that old problem again. By then, I knew the governor was also against my appointment, and he stopped answering my calls.

I met with Bashir and some of the radio team and other activists. Bashir thought we should be patient, bide our time and wait for the fuss to calm down. But then we heard that a much bigger demonstration against me was being organised, by the influential market trader, the same one who was organising for revenues to go to the Taliban. He was insisting that the ex-Taliban commander was the rightful winner of the post, and that nobody in the city wanted me. He had managed to rouse quite a crowd, who had set up a tent as their HQ inside the governor's compound, close to the gate of the municipality office, and also blocked the main road to Kabul.

When the governor continued to refuse my calls, I decided: 'Enough is enough. I'll go to his office myself.'

Ignoring the crowd, I headed straight inside the building to find that the governor had left. His deputy told me to go home and wait a few more days.

'We're working on it,' he said.

I didn't believe him, resolving to return to the office every day until the governor announced my appointment, just to get me off his case. I turned and huffed back down the stairs, and as I stepped out into the sunshine, a roar went up in the crowd gathered outside, as if someone had turned a volume dial up. The shock of it stopped me dead, and I stood and stared out at these men who were shouting about me as if I couldn't hear or answer back.

'Why is she here?' one old man shouted. 'We don't want her! She's not allowed to enter this office.'

Two men with white beards started coming towards me with sticks raised in their hands. Others were egging on children who were reaching down to scoop up stones. I suddenly realised they were going to attack me – this crowd of men who had been shouting all day about immorality! For a second longer I froze on the steps, staring out into the twisted faces. Then I heard the deputy governor shouting behind me.

'Miss Ghafari, come back inside!'

He might not have wanted me as mayor, but he also didn't want to see me dead on the doorstep. The police guarding the governor's office locked the doors against the mob, and called the district police chief. They sent two Humvees to accompany us back to Kabul. By the time they arrived, minutes later, the mob was really angry. Some of them were carrying banners printed with a photo of me and Bashir that was taken at our engagement, surrounded by a red circle and with a red line crossing out our faces. There was something comical about the fact that they had chosen a photo of me at my most beautiful; I appreciated it. I took a deep breath, and braced myself. Surrounded by a ring of police officers, with our heads hunched down, we hurried to my waiting car and I dived into the back seat. At the same moment a rock smashed through one of the windows, sending pieces of glass into my forehead. The police looked terrified. Blood dripped down my face as the driver pulled off, edging through the crowd that wanted to kill me: the people I had been appointed to serve and lead.

Police Humvees escorted us back to Kabul, and I laughed all the way. As the blood dripped down onto my headscarf, I felt a mixture of nervous relief at my lucky escape, and genuine amazement at the stupidity of the men of Maidan Shahr.

In Kabul, I lobbied anyone who would listen. Some of the civil servants told me that nobody in Wardak wanted me as mayor, although I knew it was just a few people – the land mafia, revenue thieves, and the corrupt leaders of the provincial government – who were making a lot of noise. I watched others who had gone through the same round of examinations as I had being appointed to their provinces and starting their jobs. Meanwhile, there was a big outrage about a Hazara man, a member of a persecuted minority, who had been denied a place at the military university, even though he had scored high marks in the entrance exam. There was such an outcry about it that, within days, he had been invited to meet the deputy president and was offered his place at the university. His situation was similar to mine, yet it had been sorted out almost immediately. Eventually, I couldn't hold back any longer. One evening, I opened my Facebook and began drafting a post about everything that was happening to me.

'If nobody is going to give me my rights, then take away my Afghan identity card,' I wrote. 'I will find another country in which I am safe and my rights as a woman are respected.'

I hit the post button, and sat back. Within minutes, people started liking and commenting, sharing their indignation at what was happening to me. Their support invigorated me, and over the next few days I started talking to all the local media who were willing to tell my story, and also discovered who was involved with the smear campaign: Ghulam Mohamad, the brother of one of President Ghani's advisors. Ghulam Mohamad had also been in jail for supporting the Taliban. I knew this was a scoop, and took my evidence to TOLO TV, the news channel in Afghanistan with the most editorial independence and the bravest journalists. Almost immediately after they ran the story, the head of the directorate of local governance, the department that oversees regional municipalities, called me and told me that I could go to Wardak with one of their directors and be announced as mayor. Success!

We drove to Maidan Shahr the next morning. The

directorate had kept my arrival a secret to prevent more protests, but someone found out. A crowd formed inside the municipality compound again, and this time they were carrying guns. They had locked the gates of the compound. I couldn't believe this was happening again. Anger swelled in my stomach.

'Why are you doing this? What is your problem?' I asked a man with a long black beard who was standing just behind the gate.

He wouldn't even look me in the eye.

'I'm not talking to this woman. Tell her not to talk to me,' he said to the official who had come with me from Kabul.

We returned to the governor's office. I wanted answers from him – he was one of the main people keeping me from my job. I knew already that he was worried about outsiders coming into the office – during his time in office, some local interests had Maidan Shahr sewn up, giving them total freedom to embezzle and to steal land. But the governor wanted to make it seem as though he was concerned about me.

'Why are you asking for this job?' he said. 'The officers in this municipality all are from Maidan Shahr, and you're a woman. If they harass you, it'll be a big shame, and I'm sure they'll do this to break you into pieces.'

'Please mind your language when you're speaking with a woman!' I retorted. 'I have high morals, strong arms and great ideas. Nobody can do this to me!'

These men, who had become so comfortable in occupying positions of power on the basis of their gender rather than their talent, were terrified at the prospect of their dominance being threatened. But it was also about a far deeper rot that had set into Afghan politics. The decree stating that I was to be appointed mayor of Wardak had come from the president, the highest authority in the country. Yet his order was being overturned by lower bureaucrats and regional chieftains. This was one of the biggest problems facing Afghanistan, years after the Taliban had been shoved out of power. There were rules and procedures, and a constitution that should have been applied to the whole country, yet they could be overturned by anyone who wielded a gun. Every Afghan man thinks he is the president of his own area, be it his house, his tribe or his town, and that his law comes before the law of the land.

In a final attempt to expel me, the media team of the directorate of local governance posted an announcement on their official Facebook page: 'By the agreement of Zarifa Ghafari we are sending her to another position. We will announce a new mayor for the province.'

Agreement? I had never agreed to such a thing. In fact, I had done the opposite: I had told the officials that if they were not going to allow me to take up my job in Wardak, then I would not accept any job in the government at all. And who was the person they intended to appoint as mayor instead of me? The candidate who was a member of Hekmatyar's party. This was my breaking point. I began considering something drastic.

I told nobody, not even Bashir, that I was thinking about self-immolation. The thought of it terrified me: how would I feel as I poured the petrol over myself and then struck the match? Would I be able to go through with it? Would I scream in regret and agony in my final moments? But I also knew that history and traditions are changed by people who are willing to sacrifice themselves for the good of everyone who comes after them. I wanted to see the injustices of this country finished, for ever, and if I had to end my own life to do that, it was a price I was ready to pay. I had been passed the number of Hamdullah Mohib, an advisor to the national security council and a direct line to the president. I cried down the line as I told Mohib that I was planning to set fire to myself in front of the presidential palace. My tears were not fake, and my threat was not empty. If I couldn't take up my position, then I would at least make sure that everyone in the world knew about the injustices in my country.

'Wait!' he told me. 'Don't do that.' He promised that he would speak directly to Matin Bek, the head of the directorate of local governance.

Finally, people in positions of power were paying as much attention to my situation as the public were. It took my threat of violence against myself to meet the strength of the mobs who wanted to hurt me. I also had to use my connections, like anyone who wants to get things done in Afghanistan. I went through the contact list on my phone, trying to find anyone else who might listen. Finally, I found a number for Wali Khan Basharmal, a member of President Ghani's office. I called him and repeated my threat to set fire to myself. He told me to write and send a letter to him, and that he would print it off and hand it to the president himself. Here is what I wrote:

It has been nine months of struggle. This is my right, but it is just my gender that is stopping me from taking office. It is not a crime to be a woman. If there is a decree from the president, how can mafias and warlords stop this decree from being enacted? What is going on in this country? Is this the situation for everyone, or just for women? Why has our system not developed better than this? The directorate of local governance is refusing to help me, simply because I am a woman. If this happens to me I will set myself on fire. It will be a lesson for everyone, so that they will think about this before they do the same to any other woman.

Basharmal followed through on his promise. In April 2019, the president instructed the directorate of local governance to announce my appointment. They did so at two o'clock that same afternoon. I was – at last – officially the mayor.

The Wardak governor's face was sour as a pickled lemon as he read out the official announcement. Afterwards, he told me to go home for a few days so that he could talk to all the municipality workers and tell them they had to accept me. I waited for two days in Kabul with no news. On the third day, I returned to Maidan Shahr, taking a journalist with me. She wanted to write a story about me, and my plan was to do an interview with her in my office, then leave; however, when we arrived, the office was locked and no one would bring me the key. The municipal staff, who were in charge of overseeing tax collections and other bureaucratic duties, had gone on strike, and refused to cooperate. The governor was furious – not with them, but with me.

'Why did you come?' he shouted down the phone as the journalist and I sat in the anteroom. 'I told you to wait.'

News of my arrival spread and by the time we made our way back outside, the striking workers had locked the gate of the municipality compound and pinned a notice to it.

'We don't want this woman as mayor for three reasons,' it read. 'Firstly, she is a young girl. Secondly, she did not win this position. And thirdly, she is not from Maidan Shahr but from Wardak.'

Nobody expected me to keep coming back, but they underestimated how stubborn I am. Five days later I returned, and this time, nobody was going to force me out. If any of the municipality staff had a problem with me, they were free to resign. I found the caretakers and guards, and instructed them to gather all the officers for a meeting where I sat at the head of the table, the sole woman in a room full of men. I could immediately pick out the ones who were the most unhappy: they glowered under their heavy, furrowed brows. I knew that the majority of them had participated in the smear campaign, and had taken part in the protest on the first day I came to the office. Yet, when I confronted them, they sat quiet, like naughty children.

'I am now responsible for this office,' I began, as they shuffled their feet and looked down at the table. 'I promise you that I will not leave until you are sick of me. I will not tolerate any of the things that have been happening. Everyone must be at their desks on time, and carry out their work properly. And I don't care about the conflict between Maidan Shahr and Wardak – I'm not responsible for that.'

One of them finally spoke up. 'But we're afraid of this conflict,' he said. 'We think you're going to sack us all because we're from Maidan Shahr, and you're from Wardak.'

'That is not what I'm going to sack anyone for,' I replied. 'I only care about whether you're qualified, and if you're doing your jobs properly. Those of you who work hard will be rewarded, but if you create problems and gossip, I won't tolerate it.'

I was determined to reform the city from the inside out, starting by stamping out the corruption inside the municipality, which had been employing some people for fifteen years, even though they were openly taking bribes. Most were connected with the various mafias in the city, or with the Taliban. At the start, I felt it was right to give them a chance. I tried the soft approach, telling them I was their colleague and that since I was new in the job, I could learn from their experience. The flattery did not work. After six months, I realised they thought I was stupid. I had tried shifting people to different jobs to see if that would prod them into working properly. Every time I did so I would receive calls from powerful people in the province, who tried to persuade me to put them back in their original roles. I tried to play the diplomat, telling them that I was moving them because they were so intelligent, and their skills were needed temporarily elsewhere. Nothing changed. They carried on exactly as they had done before – taking bribes, slacking off and back-biting. I heard from my sources in the city that they were going out into the tea shops and telling anyone who would listen that I was a fool.

The only way to deal with this was with an iron hand. I called another meeting, this time of the entire municipality staff from the bureaucrats down to the street cleaners. There were nearly one hundred people gathered in front of me. Just one of them was a woman, an older lady who worked in the human resources department.

'Nothing has changed and this municipality is still not functioning,' I told them. 'So, I'm going to start changing your positions. Everybody who has completed their original term of employment must sit an entrance test for their position. Some council roles will be opened up to the popular vote.'

There was a muttering and shuffling in the audience. Many of them knew they would not win their jobs back. I guessed that some of them could not even be bothered to try, which was fine by me. By now I had worked out who the decent people were – mostly those in the lower positions, like the street cleaners and the caretakers, those who were honest and hardworking, and who had supported me when I took office even if they were unaccustomed to working for a woman. They would be welcomed. But the higher-level officers were largely corrupt, and mostly related – they were all cousins! It was like working for a family business, not a government office. Officials in the department in charge of land management were asking for money in order to issue documents that should have been free, I discovered. One advised me, entirely straight-faced, that I should pay off the locals who were protesting against me. I couldn't work with such people. The incumbents had been so busy protesting against me in the first months that I was mayor that they had neglected to do any of the paperwork for that year's budget. I was going to bring in a whole new generation of workers, who did not have such strong bonds with the criminals and who would bring fresh energy and ideas to their roles.

Winning over my colleagues was only the first part of the challenge; I also had to win over the people I was serving. Several times a week, from my first day in the post, I ventured into the city and spoke with as many people as I could. The population was just 15,000 in Maidan Shahr, and I already had a large network there thanks to the radio station. But the total population across Wardak was more than half a million people, most of them living in villages where the Taliban was in full or partial control. As dangerous as it was, I knew that I had to get out there to introduce myself to these people as their mayor, and let them know that they could come to me if they had any problems. Together with Masoom, my bodyguard, and often with a village elder or mullah by my side, we drove out to tiny settlements of mud-brick houses, places of wretched poverty set amid stunning mountain landscapes. Although I was working for everyone in Wardak, I was particularly concerned about the plight of the women in these places. Many had lost their husbands, either to Taliban attacks or to American bombs. In either case, the result was the same: they were left alone, with no income and no way to earn money and feed their children. Furthermore, many were terrified that, once their sons became teenagers, they would be lured by the extremists' seductive promises of revenge and paradise. In fact, the Taliban did little for these places, and particularly for these women; the group's social programmes consisted of setting up religious schools, and claiming that Allah would provide the rest. Men might have been fooled by that, thinking it was at least more than the government gave them, but these women certainly weren't. As I sat alone with them, they cursed the Taliban, for all the misery it had brought upon them. In those meetings, I held back my tears. My role was to be the strong one, a woman they believed was powerful enough to change their situation. But back in my office, behind my closed door, I would often break down and weep.

Back in Maidan Shahr, my first target was licensing revenues. In my plan for the city I had estimated that of the more than three hundred businesses operating, only eighteen had licences. Again, I tried the soft approach first. I went out and spoke to the owners, telling them they had to come into the municipality offices to file the proper paperwork. A week later, only ten of them had done so. I had learned from my experience with my colleagues – now I needed to be tough. I gathered the licensing team, and together we walked out into the centre of Maidan Shahr. We worked our way through every shop in the market, down one side of the road and then back up the other. In each one, I asked them to show their licence, and if they didn't have it I asked them to step outside. Each one had an excuse. Some claimed that they had applied for the licence but that it hadn't arrived. Others said they weren't earning enough to buy one. That was a lie – the most expensive business licence in this city cost 2,500 Afghani, a fraction of what even a small business would make in a week. The more creative among them showed me old licences and hoped I wouldn't notice that they were years out of date.

Others laughed in my face. It had simply become a habit that the people of this region did not pay their taxes. I did not care. Every time a premises could not show their licence, I ordered them to close, put a notice on their door, and told them that they could reopen when they came back with the correct paperwork. Then as I was driving back to Kabul, I saw to my outrage that all of them had opened up again. Two days later I went back into the market, but this time with a police officer at my side – the sole woman on the streets of Maidan Shahr, striding down the pavement with a team of men at my command. I told the disobedient shop owners that if they opened again without a licence, they would be prosecuted. This did the trick. Soon, the begrudging shopkeepers were filing into the municipality offices. I kept up my visits to the ones who were still refusing, two or three times a week until they gave in. Three months after I started, all the businesses in the city were licensed and paying rates.

Next I turned to the land mafias. Thanks to all the unused spaces hoarded by the land-grabbers, new buildings were being constructed on land that was entirely unsuitable. In the market, one restaurant owner was expanding his premises onto a public footpath. I had already sent my staff to tell him he could not do that, but he continued anyway. By the time I showed up at his door, the extension was completed, jutting out over the pedestrianised area and blocking a storm drain. He had assumed that I would just let it go once the work was done.

'Miss Mayor, I have spent money on this!' he pleaded.

I might have felt sympathetic had I not already warned him. The same day I asked the demolition team to go with me and ordered the bulldozer operator to tear the roof off the illegal extension, watching from the pavement with my arms folded as the huge yellow arm ripped it from the walls.

'You have two days to take down the rest!' I told the owner, who was staring open-mouthed as his roof crashed to the ground.

The rest of the market traders had come out of their shops to watch, some muttering behind their hands but others clearly impressed that a tiny woman had the nerve to do this. I was determined that by the time I was finished, they would be more scared of me with my clipboard and records than they were of the Taliban with their guns.

I took some pictures of the scene and posted them onto the municipality's Facebook account.

'This is what will happen to anyone who is building illegally,' I wrote.

I was not only Wardak's first female mayor – I was also its most stylish. Among a sea of men dressed in shades of beige and monochromes, and often sporting the same long beards, I stood out in my delicately patterned dresses and headscarves. In my portrait at the top of the official pyramid on the wall of the municipal compound in Maidan Shahr, I wore a maroon headscarf and a serene half-smile. My Kabul outfits of jeans and casual sweaters simply wouldn't cut it here. That was partly because of the conservatism of the place – a woman in jeans would cause a small riot in Maidan Shahr. But I also realised that I needed to develop a certain persona in order to survive in this role. It was no use simply trying to pretend I was 'one of the boys'. I had to turn my femininity to my advantage, without ever making it look like a weakness. Had I been working as a mayor in the West I would have channelled Hillary Clinton with sharp trouser suits and killer jewellery. My Maidan Shahr version of that was chicly cut long dresses with detailing around the waistband and cuffs, in deep navy blue or delicate pastel pink, teamed with coordinating headscarves. Every inch of skin down to my wrists was covered, and only the smallest amount of hair showed under my scarf. I made sure that nobody could ever accuse me of being dressed inappropriately.

Yet, of course, they did. The governor gossiped, claiming that I was going out in short dresses and tiny scarves. At each meeting he held with other provincial officials, I was told that he brought up the issue of my outfits and that behind my back, he kept claiming that I was not doing my job properly and asking that I be investigated. One day I discovered a new construction site, where a building was going up without proper safeguards – even I could see that the foundations were nowhere near deep enough. I sent my team out to check, and sure enough it was unsound. The bulldozer went in, and down it came. But when I checked who the land it was being built on belonged to, I was stunned. I was told it was the governor's!

I had stayed mostly silent up to this point, choosing to ignore his attacks on me in favour of just getting on with my job. I suspected that contracts from his department were going to people connected to the Taliban. But this was too much. I called him. As usual he did not answer. I wrote him a long message on WhatsApp:

I know that you sit at every meeting talking against me and commenting on the length of my skirt. But I'm shocked. Who are you to say this? You sit at every meeting saying that I'm not a capable mayor. Why? Because I refuse to take part in your corruption or give you a chance to grab more land. Take care of your own corrupt team and broken office.

It was infuriating, but at the same time satisfying. Here was proof that I was the one doing my job properly, and the true reason why they were scared of me. Soon after, the governor left his post; I assumed his behaviour had grown too wild even for the Afghan government to ignore.

A large part of my job as mayor was receiving people in my office. Hospitality is a large part of Afghan culture – no deal can be done nor meeting start without an initial twenty minutes of tea and small talk. Mullahs, local leaders, businessmen and ordinary citizens came in and out every day, making representations or simply asking for my help in solving their problems. The ones I might have expected to be the most hostile to me, the mullahs, were actually some of the kindest. One of the religious leaders of Wardak, Mavlavi Azizulrahman Seddiqi, actually knew about Islam, and knew it could (and should) be used as a force for good, rather than to oppress. He would often visit my office with other mullahs accompanying him. We would sit for many hours talking about the city, its problems, and what needed to be done to make Afghanistan a better country.

My office, though, definitely needed a woman's touch.

Me on my first birthday, taken in one of Kabul's professional photography studios. At that time I knew nothing about the troubles my country was going through — that's why I have a big smile on my face.

Me on my third birthday, also taken at one of Kabul's photography studios. It was the tradition in my family that we would be gifted new clothes on our birthdays, and then have our portraits taken.

Me with my dad, shortly after the fall of the Taliban in 2001. My aunt, who lives in Germany, brought us a Canon camera as a present, and my mother took this photograph on it.

Protesting for justice for Farkhunda Malikzada, an Afghan woman who was killed by a mob in Kabul in 2015. I organised a petition in Chandigarh, India, where I was studying at the time, and under global pressure the Afghan authorities brought prosecutions against her killers.

When my colleagues protested against me as mayor, women entered my office with slogans in support of me and my work.

When I finally managed to take up my position as mayor, one of the first visitors I received in my office was my father. It was a very happy moment for me, when I finally saw that he was proud of what I have achieved.

Marking International Girl Child Day with orphans in Maidan Shahr. I always hope that when little Afghan girls meet me, they see that they can be something more than our society tells them they can.

Discussing the budget for city development with the staff at Wardak municipality. They were not used to taking orders from a woman, but I wanted to lead by example and win their respect.

Visiting the only park for women in Wardak to make it a greener, safer place for women. I wanted to help them get out of the house for a picnic with their families, something that's very hard to do.

One of the hardest moments of my life: visiting my father's grave on 6 November 2020, the day after he was murdered. I placed the Afghan flag over the top, and promised him that I would keep working for our country.

Two days before the fall of the government to the Taliban, I was working in the defence ministry and went to visit the internal refugees' camp in Kabul. Streets were full of displaced people from several provinces and I walked all day to find the families of martyrs, disabled soldiers and prisoners of war. Everyone was desperate for help, and eventually I couldn't help but sit and cry.

Handing out aid packages in Dasht-e Barchi, a Hazara area of Kabul, in February 2022. After the Taliban retook the country, international aid organisations pulled out and the country came under sanctions, plunging many more people into poverty.

Meeting children in Changa, a remote village in Wardak province, where the only school is a single room for the boys, and an open courtyard for girls. These villages have seen little of the billions that poured into Afghanistan between 2001 and 2021, and they are the Taliban's strongholds.

When I met the women seeking support from APAW I always
listened to their stories and tried to help.

Meeting women taking sewing lessons at my centre in Kabul. Making clothes is a great way for
women to make money – you do not have to be literate, and you can do it from home.

Meeting Angela Merkel on 9 September 2021, a few weeks after the Taliban takeover.
We spent more than an hour discussing the situation in Afghanistan, and what steps
the international community needs to take to help the people there.

Me, sitting by Qargha reservoir, during my trip back to Afghanistan in February 2022.
It is one of the places that I miss most in my country.

When I moved in the paintwork was dirty grey and the curtains a depressing shade of dark green. There were no cushions on the sofas, nothing to make you feel as if it was a place where you could relax and hold a conversation. I set about decorating it immediately, buying new white curtains that let bright sunlight filter through, and repainting the walls in a delicate magnolia. I got rid of the heavy dark wood furniture and brought in a light wooden desk. On it I placed the flag of Afghanistan, next to the pale blue flag of the municipality.

Soon I was receiving visitors from outside Wardak, too. Ironically, all the attempts to stop me taking up my position had turned me into a minor celebrity with a reach way beyond my office. One of the first international news stories about me was published in the *New York Times*. One of their correspondents had heard about my battle to become mayor, and asked if he could write an article about it. After that, the interest in my story exploded. I was receiving requests almost daily to do more interviews with other international media outlets, and soon other invitations started flooding in too, from important people around the world. I realised that my fight to become mayor had given me a platform far bigger than anything I had had before. In Turkey, I met President Erdoğan and his wife Emine in their huge palace in Ankara. I met government officials in Sweden and India, and was invited to speak at conferences, in front of audiences made up of the world's most influential people.

But the support that meant most to me came from closer to home. One day, not long after I had taken office, I heard a commotion outside in the corridor. I had made a new rule – no guns were to be brought into municipality buildings. It was not just about security. This was to be a civilised place, where if people fought they did so with words, not weapons. It quickly changed the atmosphere, and demolished the hierarchy of violence that promotes men with guns to the top. But now, someone was trying to bring their weapon inside.

'The officer won't give me his gun,' someone said.

Soldiers, who were allowed to take their guns into the mosques and keep their shoes on as they prayed, were banned from doing so in my offices, a rule that especially applied to those I did not know personally. I stormed out, ready to confront him. When I saw who it was, I burst out laughing.

'This is my father!'

He had come to congratulate me, for winning the race, and for persevering until I took up the position. He had brought three of his army colleagues with him. I knew then that he was proud of me, after all those years of fighting each other. I invited him in and ordered tea as he handed me a bunch of flowers. I could barely keep the tears from my eyes as we posed together for a photo: my dad and his daughter, now mayor of his home province, in front of the Afghan flag.

Six

February 2022

Maidan Shahr

The Alpha Market was open for business, sign blinking proudly at the edge of the car park it had been built on.

'I blocked that construction!' I shouted to nobody in particular as the market flashed past the car window. 'When I was mayor I blocked it because it was illegal, and now look!'

It was an eerie feeling to return to the city I had served and then fled. On one level, not much had changed. The huge checkpoint at the entrance to the city still created a backlog of traffic, only now it was worse because the Taliban soldiers manning it paused to pray five times a day. The military bases looked the same, and it was only if you peered closely that you could see that the occupants had changed. Finally, some repairs were being done on the main road, huge steamrollers flattening out the fresh tarmac that was being poured into the old bomb craters. But I also noticed that there was now litter lining the verges, hundreds of plastic bags waving gently like surrender flags in the breeze. The air was horribly dirty, thick with fumes belched out by the lorries waiting at the checkpoint. And there was a building boom underway. The Taliban had appointed their man as mayor – someone who had been collecting protection money from the city's businesses for years on their behalf. He had unplugged the stoppages on illegal construction that I had put in place during my tenure, and now the city was slipping back towards being the dirty, unorganised place I had taken over.

It had been a daily, street-level struggle to make the progress I had in Maidan Shahr. When I started a campaign to clear rubbish from the streets and get people to stop throwing their waste onto the ground, I went out there myself with a litter picker and bin bag. The people of Wardak were so used to the hands-off approach of other municipal leaders that I presented an absurd figure. I've no doubt that some thought I had finally learned my place as a woman – not behind a desk issuing orders, but clearing up after them. Yet even as I inched through the streets clearing rubbish, all the time encouraging people to do the same, an old man sat outside his shop peeling potatoes and throwing the skins into the street. He had the gall to do it right in front of me, and moreover he was laughing in my face.

'Come here and clean up the mess you are making!' I shouted.

'I'll do it later,' he chuckled, winking to his gang of friends, who were now also laughing.

I squared my shoulders and fixed him with the look I used on my little brothers when they misbehaved: 'No, not later. Now!'

Suddenly, he didn't know what to do. He saw that I wasn't going to back down – and by then the whole city knew that I was a woman who was ready to tear down illegal buildings and close businesses that weren't operating legally.

'Do you have any gloves?' he asked.

'You weren't wearing gloves when you threw it down here ten seconds ago,' I replied. With a furious sideways glance, he came out, and picked up the skins.

The litter on the streets of Maidan Shahr, less than a year after I had left office, bothered me to the point where I wanted to jump out of the car and start ordering people to pick it up again. It was as if I had worked for two years for nothing: I could have accepted no longer being mayor if I knew that at least I had left some legacy. But at the same time, I had an urge to get out of this place as fast as possible. As we drove towards the checkpoint, me in the back seat with a face mask pulled up right over my nose, my anxiety kicked back in like a reflex. When I strode out onto the streets of Maidan Shahr as the mayor of Wardak, commanding bulldozers and issuing penalties, no one could have guessed that I was constantly thinking about my safety. Usually I had no security guards or police officers beside me, just my team from the municipality. I was determined not to show any fear, yet I never allowed myself to feel too comfortable. The Taliban was always close, nestled in the valleys but also walking in the city, blending in with everyone else. When Kabul fell in 2001, Wardak was the natural place for Taliban fighters to retreat to: close to the city, deeply conservative, and with scores of supporters among its citizens, its tentacles reaching into the business sector, local government and security structures. For a woman to become a local celebrity and then mayor of a place like Wardak was already an affront. The fact that I had taken such deliberate steps to clear the municipality of corruption was even worse.

Now, driving back through the city I had once governed, I knew that somewhere on these streets, maybe manning a checkpoint or observing from one of the watchtowers, were the men who had once tried to kill me.

Even after Bashir and I were engaged, Afghan tradition meant that we couldn't live together until we were married. The neighbours would have gossiped about us, scandal that would have reached my family, who didn't deserve the embarrassment it would cause them. I still lived alone in my flat in Kabul. I had also hired a lady to help me take care of the house, a widow whose grown children had fled the nest. It was partly a favour to her, but it was also good to have someone around to do the chores since I left for work early every day and came home late when I took up my post in Wardak. The commute was dangerous, but it would have been even more perilous for me to stay overnight. Whatever security there was in the daytime in Maidan Shahr was fleeting; at night, the city was the domain of men who lurked in the shadows. I had an itchy sensation of being watched wherever I went there. Masoom, my driver and bodyguard, often pleaded with me to leave early, or to not go in on certain days. My answer was always the same: *Allah is kind*. But there would be no divine intervention to stop an assassin's bullet if it was marked for me.

In November 2019, only weeks after I had officially taken up my post, I travelled to the city of Mazar-e Sharif to attend my cousin's wedding. It was a joyful couple of days, and one of the first times that I forgot about work and was able to relax since I had applied to become mayor. We danced and congratulated the new couple, and I caught up with all the cousins and aunties I had not seen in months or years. Now that I had proved everyone wrong and risen to a position of actual power, I sensed a respect from my family that I had never felt before. Of course, I always knew that they loved me, but there was nobody who really understood why I was fighting so hard for a different kind of life. Sometimes, that turned into outright hostility, like all the fights I had with my father as a teenager. Mostly, though, it manifested as a kind of awkwardness, my distant female relatives not knowing how they should communicate with me. Now, their questions flowed. They wanted to know what it was like to sit in an office and dole out orders to men, and how I felt when I was finally announced as mayor. I told them that in that moment I was thinking of them, and all the other young women in Afghanistan, and how I might be the first to do something like this but I certainly wouldn't be the last. It was always an affecting feeling, to see curiosity in women's eyes tinged not with disdain but with ambition when they looked at me. I always hoped that, wherever I went as mayor, there were little girls looking at me and thinking: *Well hang on, if this woman can do it, then why can't I?*

Everyone begged me to stay longer at the wedding, but on the second evening I had to return to Kabul. I was due to fly to Tbilisi, the Georgian capital, with a big delegation two days later. I needed to sort out some paperwork and make sure that everything would run smoothly in my absence. I also needed to wash my hair and shower, but when I let myself into the flat it was dark and the electricity was off. I could also detect a faint smell of gas, which is nothing too unusual in Kabul apartments. Even newly built blocks don't tend to be connected to a mains supply; instead, we all bought gas in big metal canisters, which we connected to our stoves with rubber piping. I opened the window, and turned to the stove.

The second I clicked the lighter, a huge flame leapt from the stove and shot along the rubber pipe. Instinctively I jerked my head back so that the fire would not catch in my hair, at the same time turning the gas back off at the stove. The flame died down, almost as quickly as it had shot up. My heart was thumping but I felt the blood come back to my face.

That was a lucky escape.

Then I felt a creeping heat in my right foot. I had been so focused on the flames on the stove top that I hadn't noticed the fire reach the canister. Gas was leaking out of the top of it – the smell I had noticed when I came into the kitchen – and now it was on fire. Already, it had caught the hem of my synthetic pyjama bottoms and was creeping up the leg. I went into autopilot: the shock was more intense than the

162

pain. I began patting at the fire by my ankle, thinking that I could easily put it out. But seconds later the flames had also caught the other leg of my pyjamas and the sleeves of my top. Now panic set in. I realised that I was really on fire. I flung open the door of my apartment, and stumbled blindly into the hallway.

Bashir arrived just at that moment. He had been on his way over; we had planned to discuss my trip to Georgia. He heard my increasingly wild screams and ran up the stairs, the smell of my burning skin and synthetics filling him with terror. I didn't feel any pain, just heat. But the flames were like a beast crawling up my body, and with smoke surrounding me I couldn't even see my way across the hallway to where a bucket of water sat in the dark. Wrapped inside my messy panic was a core of cold hard logic.

You're going to die, it told me. *If you don't put these flames out in the next seconds they're going to consume and kill you.*

Bashir ran to me, trying to pat out the flames. He didn't stop even when the fire started scorching his own hands, but it had taken too firm of a grip on me to be put out.

'Water!' I screamed, motioning to the bucket. 'Throw the water over me.'

In the next second the fire was out, and I stood there dripping wet and dazed. A putrid black smoke rose from my feet. Then, like a thunder clap, the agony, as if a fanged dog was tearing chunks of flesh from me, with acid then poured onto the wounds. And then just as suddenly I was so cold, as if the water Bashir tipped over me had hardened to ice. I was shivering uncontrollably, and started to cry now from the pain. The skin on my feet and hands looked like a melted plastic bottle, all twists and valleys, and an angry, terrifying red. I took the remains of my burnt pyjamas off me, and put on a loose shirt and trousers. The whole of the kitchen was blackened with soot: I had not realised how intense the flames were. Together we drove to the hospital, Bashir wincing in pain as the burns on his hands made contact with the steering wheel, and me trying to hold in the vomit as my pain reached a crescendo. When I tried to put on my shoes I saw my burnt skin hanging off my feet.

We could have gone to the military hospital, where I would have received good treatment on account of my father's service in the army. But all of my family were still celebrating in Mazar-e Sharif, and I knew someone would call my father the minute I was admitted. So instead we drove to the nearest private hospital. All I could think of was the pain; I was pleading with the nurses for painkillers. It did not even occur to me that this was not a specialist burns hospital. In one look, the doctor knew my injuries were too serious for him to deal with. He sent us immediately to another hospital, the Istiqlal, a low-rise yellow building that had become the go-to place for Kabulis caught in bomb blasts. Perversely, it also housed one of the city's biggest maternity units: a place of birth and unnatural death, all under one roof.

By the time we reached the Istiqlal, the painkillers had kicked in and I noticed the burns on Bashir's face and hands. I told him, as I was being wheeled into the operating theatre, that he needed to get himself treated, too. The last thing I remember before the anaesthetic hit was my sense of relief that I soon wouldn't be able to feel anything, and shock at just how young the surgeons looked. Most of them were interns, still training. Afghanistan does not have many experienced doctors, even for someone whose skin has melted off.

I awoke in a room filled with screaming. My bed was one of ten on the ward, each one occupied by a woman in soul-wrenching pain. One was just a young girl – she had fallen into a tandoor oven and 60 per cent of her body was covered in burns. She only ever paused for a few seconds between her cries.

An unusually large number of Afghan women are admitted to burns units. Unlike my injuries, most of theirs are not accidental. I realised the irony of my situation, even as I lay there in mind-bending pain: only a few months earlier, I too had threatened to do this to myself. Self-immolation is a common suicide method for women who have few other means to kill themselves. Usually they have been locked in their homes, abused and enslaved by their husbands or fathers, and use the gas to their cooking stoves to set themselves alight. Others are burned by the jealous men in their lives, who accuse them of affairs or of bringing dishonour to the family. Some men simply want to make their wives unattractive so that no other man will look at her. Sometimes they burn their wives with fire, other times with acid. The women, if they survive, become pariahs, marked for ever by their wounds. Suicide is hugely shameful in Muslim cultures, as is betraying your husband. So even though the fault lies with men and the women bear the physical agony, the blame is heaped on them too. Usually they are kept inside by their families or hide themselves away. It is only the doctors in the burns units who really know the extent of their suffering.

I was still in searing pain. Under the bandages on my hands and feet it felt as if razor blades were grazing what was left of my skin. I could barely move, the unburnt parts of me still heavy from the anaesthetic. A black shape moving at the bottom of my bed caught my eye. Glancing down, I saw a cockroach scuttling by my foot. I was revolted, but there was nothing I could do. Every time I tried to move something, it felt as if the razors scraped deeper.

My mind started racing, desperate to escape the pain, this place, the child's cries which sounded like my own the night before. *I'll take my records and go to India*, I thought manically, *to the hospital that treated me after my accident there.*

I called one of the nurses over.

'I'm leaving!' I told her. 'Please, give me my documents.'

She refused.

What could I do? I was incapacitated, crippled with pain and medication. Thankfully, the doctor in charge of the unit saw how distraught I was, and, after a long discussion, arranged for me to be moved into a separate room, where my family and friends could visit me.

On the second day the doctors told me they were going to change my dressings and clean my wounds. The bandages were stuck to my raw skin, and when they started to pull off the gauze with tweezers it sent a new shockwave of pain to my core. With every bandage they pulled off it felt as though they were taking another layer of my skin with it. I screamed as hard as I had the night I was on fire. In fact, this pain was worse. When they had finished, the nurse told me to put my hands next to my feet, and started pouring water over me. Not sterilised water, just the water

166

from the tap. At the same time, a foul yellowish liquid was seeping from my wounds, smelling like decay. Agony and disgust rolled over me in waves, minute after minute until finally she stopped, put medicated cream on my burns and then bandaged them again. We went through the same grisly ritual each morning. I didn't know it then, but the doctors were telling Bashir that they might have to amputate my right foot. The burns had penetrated to the bone.

That same morning, my mother called, wanting to wish me a safe trip to Georgia. I could hear in her voice that she was still high on the joy of my cousin's wedding, and I couldn't bear to bring her crashing back down.

'I'm at the airport,' I said, hoping the background noise of the hospital might sound similar to an airport terminal. 'We're taking off soon.'

She has never forgotten that lie. Even today, every time I tell her I'm fine she makes me swear several times over and promise that I am telling the truth. If I don't look into her eyes she won't believe me. Sometimes she makes me swear on her life.

On the sixth day in hospital I called her back. I asked her where she was, and who she was with, before I broke the news.

'Have you returned from Georgia?' she asked.

'No. I'm in the hospital. Please come, but please don't tell Dad, or anyone else.'

When she appeared at my bedside, I cried for the first time since the accident. Until then, I had only writhed and moaned in agony. She held my face tight and kissed me, carefully avoiding any contact with my burnt hands and feet, and told me to stay strong. She had arranged for me to be transferred to the military hospital the next morning. That day, they changed the dressings on my feet for the last time, with my mum just outside the room, telling me that I was brave and not to cry. I couldn't see that she was crying herself, falling apart on the other side of the door. When they finished and the pain had lessened, she begged me to tell her the truth. Was it a bomb attack, or an assassination attempt? Was I lying to her when I said it was just an accident?

I hadn't considered this but, later, it turned out that my mother was right. When the accident was formally investigated, it turned out that the woman I had employed to help me around the house, whom I had trusted completely, had been given money by someone to leave the gas leaking from the canister. That someone could have been anyone: an insurgent group, the mafia, warlords, or the Taliban. By now, I had given all of them a reason.

I stayed in the hospital for two weeks, undergoing more operations. After the final surgery was completed I couldn't bear to stay there any longer, just lying in bed all day and thinking about the pain I was in. I was terrified that the people who were so angry at my presence in the municipality would use the opportunity to usurp me in my absence. And so, despite the angry pleas of my doctor, I borrowed a wheelchair and returned to work in Maidan Shahr. I was still unable to walk on my burnt soles. My colleagues would carry me up the stairs of the office in my wheelchair, and when my wounds bled through my bandages I would change them, haphazardly, myself. Sometimes the pain was so intense that I thought I might vomit, but I never let that show on my face. I didn't want to reveal any crack that they could prise open to say that I was just a weak woman underneath. In the evenings, when I returned to Kabul, I still stayed in the hospital rather than in my flat, and every evening the nurses tried to persuade me to take some time off. The doctors saved my foot, but I needed skin grafts. I had just finished the first round when we were forced to flee Kabul in August 2021. The scars remain and have healed badly. Whenever I look at my hands or feet now I am reminded of the agony of that fire, but also of how strong I am to have survived it. Today, the scars turn red whenever my blood pressure rises, and I am unable to stand for too long without being in pain.

More than the scars, what remains with me is the advice my father gave me. When, after several days in hospital, I was finally able to open my phone, I checked social media and saw that hundreds of people were gossiping about how and why I got burned. It was rubbish: that I had made the attack up to get publicity, or had tried to kill myself with fire. When my dad found out the reason for my tears, he locked his eyes onto mine:

'If you want to work outside the house you have to accept that this is what comes with it,' he said. 'This is how it is. Societies like ours can't deal with a woman, or challenge her with their efforts and their abilities. Instead they try to break her. Harm her by harming her dignity. This is part of the game. If you can't accept it, then give up and sit at home.'

Those words shocked me out of my self-pity. My dad always knew best how to keep me fighting.

*

The road between Kabul and Maidan Shahr never became safe. In fact, during the time I was working in Wardak, first at the radio station and then as mayor, it grew more dangerous. Sometimes I would pass the remains of an attack not long after it had happened, the twisted bits of smoking metal strewn across the road and an acrid burning smell in the air. The Taliban was growing bolder, no longer just gathering in safehouses and carrying out occasional hits, but also launching complex operations to take control of large areas. In June 2018, the militants took eighty police officers hostage in the Jalriz district of Wardak and seized control of several checkpoints. By October of that year they were battling the officers in the outpost at Dasht-e-Top, where I had placed the radio antenna.

I also saw the immediate aftermath of an American airstrike. The missiles had landed in the middle of the most dangerous area, around the brick factories along the highway. They killed only civilians. When we stopped the car close to a plume of black smoke I found an old man howling that his son had been killed. It took a while for me to calm him down enough so that he could tell us what happened. His son was a labourer, not a militant, he explained, and left behind a wife and children who would have to fend for themselves. The Taliban used this area for its attacks and everybody knew it, but in times like these it felt as if the Americans were pursuing a policy of collective guilt. How were unarmed locals meant to stop hardened militants intent on using their neighbourhoods as shelter?

On another occasion, Masoom and I were travelling to the office, him with one hand on the steering wheel, the other holding the pistol that was resting in his lap. The road ahead of us was blocked with dozens of angry men. It was a demonstration: American soldiers had raided their village in the night and shot dead three brothers, none of whom had anything to do with the Taliban. We spotted one man in the crowd who certainly was Taliban, though: he pulled his scarf over his face every time he was in my eyeline. This had been going on for nearly twenty years: the Taliban on one side; the US on the other, and blameless Afghan people caught in between. For whatever progress had been made, was it worth this price? It is a question I still cannot answer.

Eventually, the US seemed willing to give up on any small gains they had made. On 29 February 2020, they signed a deal with the Taliban, agreeing to withdraw their troops. In return, the Taliban pledged to prevent terrorist groups from using Afghanistan as a base to attack America.

Five days after that deal was signed, I was in Washington, DC, standing in front of some of the most powerful people in America. In the three months since I had finally taken my office in Maidan Shahr, a paradox had emerged. At home – in Wardak and even within my own family – few people were impressed by what I was doing. But outside of Afghanistan, my profile was soaring. The BBC named me among its 100 most influential women for 2019, and I was invited to speak at film festivals, human rights forums and round tables with the decision makers in powerful countries.

I knew that all of these people wanted to use me for their own purposes. Erdoğan was keen to meet me because I am a Muslim, and because Turkey has its own interests in Afghanistan. The US wanted to tap my experience and contacts within my country. For events organisers in rich Western cities I was a vogueish addition to their billings, someone they could use to tick off their diversity boxes. But that was fine by me. If by travelling around the world and talking about my country it meant that I could alert people to what was happening there, then it was worth it. Even though my English was not perfect, I knew that I have enough charisma and passion for my subject to keep my audiences engrossed. And they were: from Geneva to Ankara, I watched the same expressions of shock and then horror on people's faces as I revealed the realities of life in Afghanistan, and warned them that things were now getting worse, not better.

In Washington, I was presented with the International Women of Courage Award by the state department, alongside eleven other brave female activists from around the world. The award was a recognition of my work in Wardak, and in my speech I thanked the US for being the world's strongest and most outspoken defender of women's rights. On stage, in my brightly coloured dress and gauzy headscarf, feeling glamorous and proud in bright red lipstick, I told them how I hoped that the little girls of Wardak, seeing me as their mayor, would believe they could grow up to be someone just as powerful. I was grateful to the US government for recognising my struggles and my achievements, and for giving a platform to an Afghan woman. But I had criticisms, as well as praise. At the end of my speech I turned to Mike Pompeo, then secretary of state, who was sitting just to my right next to then First Lady Melania Trump, and looked him in the eye as I delivered my final lines.

'Please, I ask for your support, to ensure that the Afghan peace process does not erase the gains that have been made since the dark days of the Taliban regime.'

Behind closed doors, I went further. For me, the most exciting part of this trip to Washington was not the award, nor the chance to see this famous city where so much recent history has been shaped, but the chance to meet all kinds of people within the government and inform them about Afghanistan in ways that might influence their policies. The fact that the US had just entered into this agreement with the Taliban made it even more pressing that I state my case to them: this was a rare opportunity for an Afghan woman who was fighting in the trenches to explain what that deal really meant. I set off on the trip with a list of topics that I knew I had to discuss: women's education and employment rights, maternal health, and Pakistan's continuing malign influence in my country. In every meeting I held with state department officials, I made it clear that any deal with the Taliban would drag Afghanistan back to the dark days of the 1990s, that it would be a disaster for the whole country, and a tragedy for women in particular. If there was one positive thing that had come out of America's long war in Afghanistan, it was that girls now had the right to education. Even if the number of those enrolled in school were still shockingly low, there was at least a generation who had grown up with the opportunity to dream.

I also wanted answers. If the whole purpose of sending the military into Afghanistan in 2001 was to find Osama bin Laden, why wasn't America putting more pressure on Pakistan after he was discovered there in 2011? Why did it take so long for the CIA to confirm that he was there, all the while my countrymen were dying under American bombs? As an Afghan, I understood well how Pakistan, our powerful neighbour, had meddled in my country for decades, giving succour to terrorists and allowing them free rein to cross the border and carry out their dirty work. I was shocked when I realised how few Afghans actually worked on the Afghanistan desk at the state department. There were Americans, Britons, even Pakistanis, but almost nobody who was from the country they were focusing on. No wonder they had got it so wrong. I was proud to have won the award, but profoundly depressed at the direction my country was taking. America's deal would be seen as a sign of weakness by the Taliban, almost a green light for them to step up their campaign to take over the country again. People like me would be their first targets.

I skirted death a second time just weeks after I returned from America. A small crowd of women, most of them politicians and journalists who I had met and grown close to through my work, greeted me at Kabul airport, with flowers and praise for what I had said in DC. My trip there had gained a lot of local media attention, in part because it highlighted the unusual work I was doing as a woman and because I had criticised the US deal with the Taliban. I was pleased that it had created a stir: women's voices needed to be heard on this issue; we were the ones who suffered the hardest. But I was also a mayor first, not a celebrity. As the attention quietened down, I was able to focus again on my work in Maidan Shahr.

Now, however, I was even more of a target for the Taliban. I could feel their eyes on my back.

On 22 March 2020, a Sunday, Bashir and I were driving back to Kabul in my old Ford Runner – a common civilian car the municipality provided. I had not bothered to get an armoured vehicle. It makes you stand out more, for a start, and I didn't think it was appropriate for a mayor who was shouting against corruption. Instead, we kept Bashir's handgun in the car and Masoom, my driver, carried his own Kalashnikov. We were chatting about COVID, I remember. The world had just started to take the pandemic seriously, and normal life was shutting down everywhere. In Afghanistan, always fertile soil for conspiracy theories, many people thought the virus was a Western plot. Some said that Afghans were far too tough, too macho to be bowled over by such a virus. Only weak and decadent Westerners would succumb! That was rubbish, of course. I was seriously worried about how Afghanistan, with its overcrowded, creaking health service, would cope if the virus took hold. I was wondering whether and how I should shut down my office, and how I would keep the municipality functioning.

We stopped in Spin Kalay Square, a busy hub of shops and offices in the Kampani district on the western edge of Kabul. It was one of the places being reshaped in the city's construction boom, the minarets of the old mosque dwarfed by cranes. I wanted to pick up hand sanitiser from one of the pharmacies there, and Masoom hopped out to get some. As he disappeared into the shop I heard a tapping on the side of the car, but when I looked around I couldn't see anyone. I thought one of our friends must have spotted us and was playing a joke. Then, a thin whistling past my right ear, three times: *whoosh, whoosh, whoosh.*

Bashir glanced in the side mirror. 'We're under attack!'

Just before I ducked I caught a glimpse of the barrel of a gun pointing at us from the window of a white Ford Corolla that had come up from behind. They must have followed us all the way from Maidan Shahr.

The whole thing did not last more than five minutes from start to finish, but each millisecond seemed to drag out for an hour. I can recall exactly the way Bashir's forehead furrowed when he saw our attackers, and the sharp stink of petrol that hit my nostrils when I plunged my head down into the footwell. I remember how the evening sunlight glinted off the barrel of the silenced gun, and how the chaotic square seemed to fall silent as soon as I realised that someone was trying to kill us. Everybody knew what was happening: gun violence was so common that such attacks had almost become banal.

The car carrying the shooter carried on across the square and disappeared into the rush hour. I realised that I was shaking, and in danger of throwing up. Then, with perfectly comedic timing, Masoom re-emerged from the pharmacy, his gun slung over his shoulder. He might even have been whistling as he strolled back over to the car.

'What happened?' he asked, when he saw our horrified faces.

'We were fired on!' I shouted. I was shaken and furious with Masoom: he had taken the gun with him and left us vulnerable, and even now he was clueless about what had happened.

Bashir had recovered and was determined to pursue our

attackers. He turned the key in the ignition and hit the accelerator. I let him have his way for a few minutes, as he tried to force his way through the traffic, cursing. The attackers had long disappeared. When I could see that his face had relaxed and his breathing slowed, I told him to stop and turn back. It was as if nothing had happened in Spin Kalay by the time we returned. We stopped again in front of the pharmacy and called the district police head-quarters. When the officers arrived we got out to search around and in the car. We found eight bullets: one of them had gone through the open window on Bashir's side and slammed into his headrest only moments after he ducked. Another was lodged inside the door on my side of the car.

The police might not have been interested, but the media certainly were. Some followers of mine who had heard what happened put up a post on Facebook, and within minutes it had gone viral. My mother found out when she saw me interviewed on the news. Later, when I answered her call, she was crying and shouting, furious and terrified in equal measure:

'Enough! Stop this and come home. I'm done with all of this. Nothing is more important to me than your life and safety ... Nobody here will understand or admire your efforts,' she went on. 'They'll always be trying to kill you.'

I was also shaken, even if I didn't want to show it to the cameras and my mother. How had the attackers managed to track us like that? We were always so cautious and alert to the people around us when we left Maidan Shahr, and hadn't noticed anything unusual that day. There were security cameras on the road at the gate marking the boundary between Kabul and Wardak, and I wondered if they had managed to get access to them, to know when we would be entering the city. I was even more nervous about the fact that this had happened so close to a police station, and that they had been able to disappear even though the whole area was full of checkpoints. Most of all I was angry that somebody thought they could use violence to stop me doing my work.

The staff at the municipality were amazed to see me back in the office the next day.

'Why are you here?' my assistant asked. 'You should stay at home a few more days, for your safety.'

I couldn't contemplate it. Though I had survived, staying at home would have felt like defeat.

I still didn't have an official security team, but after the attack in Spin Kalay Square the directorate of local governance decided to get me a bulletproof car, and every day when I drove to Maidan Shahr from Kabul and back again, I took two bodyguards with me. They had been provided by the directorate of security, Afghanistan's intelligence agency, after the first attempt on my life, but without weapons, so I had to find guns myself. Usually we would travel with two cars, me and Bashir in the first one, the car that had been provided by my office, and Masoom driving Bashir's car behind us with my bodyguards. It was far less than the armoured convoys and helicopters the national politicians moved about in but, if there were another attack, the guards in the car behind would be able to fire back. But Masoom couldn't help himself – like a typical Afghan driver, it was his instinct to keep overtaking us at every opportunity. I argued with him about it constantly.

If an attack happened and he was ahead of us, he might not notice until it was too late.

I had also become hyper-vigilant in crowded places. The Taliban had taken to paying beggar children to throw bombs into their targets' cars, so every time we were stuck in traffic and one approached my window I wondered if this sweet-faced child had come to kill me, together with whomever was unlucky enough to be next to me at the time. Meanwhile, I was getting weekly, sometimes twice-weekly warnings from the national directorate of security of threats they had learned of – whether it be a possible attack by men on motorcycles, or by a sticky bomb, a device fitted with powerful magnets that attaches itself to the target vehicle. Usually, they warned that the attack was going to happen in Kampani, like the previous one. Linked to many of these threats were the names of members of the Taliban in Maidan Shahr.

The commute, especially through the brick-making neighbourhood, was by far the most threatening part of my day. As we travelled the most dangerous part of the road, my stomach knotted. I imagined Taliban spotters sitting high in the mountains on either side, their binoculars trained on us. My new car also had blacked-out windows, but of course they would have worked out within days that it belonged to me. I stayed in my office in Maidan Shahr as often as I could. That was not safe, either, but now the danger of the road was overtaking it. I moved my assistant to a different office and converted his old office into my bedroom, complete with a cupboard and a small stove. In the winter months, I huddled under blankets and cooked potatoes, watching the news or looking at social media on my phone. When the weather improved I would wander into the gardens of the compound and read a book. Some evenings I even jogged around and around the building. Four guards took turns on duty outside the door of my room as the attacks from the Taliban crept closer to the city. The fighting had become nightly, the militants encroaching within five miles of Maidan Shahr.

One day early in 2021, I had to travel to my office from Kabul. We piled into the two cars and set off. As usual, I was on my phone to Masoom in the other car, arguing with him to stay behind our car. As we approached the danger stretch, I saw it: fifty metres up ahead of us, a man positioning a rocket-propelled grenade launcher at the side of the road. Even in an armoured car, this weapon would eviscerate us.

'We're under attack,' I shouted. 'Go!'

The driver slammed his foot on the accelerator and we jolted into high speed. The attacker with the RPG didn't have time to position it properly by the time we sped past him, but two more men appeared at the side of the road, one aiming a Kalashnikov at us and the other an M4 – an American-made machine gun. Both of them opened fire, letting loose a stream of bullets. In our old car we would have been dead. But even with the protection of galvanised glass and metal, I felt myself bracing for death. We sped past our attackers in seconds, yet that was enough for me to take in every detail of them, not just the type of guns they were pointing at us but the baggy fit of their shalwar khameez and how one of them had long hair curling over the top of his ears. I would be able to pick him out from a line-up by that detail, even though

I did not take in his face. The bullets were still hitting our car when they were several hundred metres behind in our rear-view mirror. Another car, which had nothing to do with us, was also hit in the attack, although luckily nobody in it was hurt.

Again, this happened in an area where security forces were close by. There was an army base fifty metres away, and few places a man with an RPG launcher would be able to hide. Yet when I called the governor to tell him what happened, he showed little interest.

'Are you safe now?' he asked.

'Yes, but they're still waiting, for sure!' I told him. 'The army can easily find them.'

The driver didn't stop until we reached the office. When we came to the main checkpoint gate of Maidan Shahr, he leant on the horn and tried to force his way through the traffic. When we finally arrived, we discovered that almost every non-armoured part of the car had been blasted by the bullets: the headlights, the wing mirrors, all just shards clinging to the frames. It was only when I made it into my office and sat behind my desk, still shaking, that the chief of police in Kabul called me. The attack had happened within his jurisdiction, and he wanted to send a team out to investigate. Now he called! Thirty minutes later! The perpetrators would be long gone, probably eating a hearty breakfast and cursing their bad luck. The police chief needed someone to show him exactly where the attack took place. And so, just as I had started to relax, I climbed back into Bashir's car (now I was sure my own car was being tracked), draped scarves over all the windows and returned to the scene of the crime. I insisted that the police chief and I go to the army base, and ask them why they had not come out to help.

As usual in Afghanistan: nobody heard or saw anything, and no one knew of any Taliban. In a country crawling with militants, nobody knew a thing.

Seven

There are two Zarifa Ghafaris. The first is the one that you will see most often, on television or leading a protest. She is tough and can seem emotionless, as if nothing in the world will throw her off course. She is confident to a level that looks arrogant, brushing off criticisms and ignoring the disapproving stares. She is the woman who is ready to battle everyone to get what she wants.

But that is not the real Zarifa. You will see who I really am at my father's graveside. It sits on a dusty hillside on the outskirts of Kabul, opposite a vehicle repair centre and next to a main road that churns with traffic. Like most cemeteries in Afghanistan this one is disorganised and poorly maintained – death is too common to be treated as special. Many of the graves are simply a pile of stones, or a sheet of tarpaulin pinned down over a mound in the earth. But a few, like my dad's, are well tended, marked with proper marble headstones and the Afghan flag. My father's grave was the first place I went when I returned to Afghanistan in February 2022; I had been so sure that I would never see it again. On the road to the cemetery I was eaten up with apprehension. What if his grave had been desecrated since the Taliban retook the country, in an act of revenge for the past twenty years? I was overjoyed to be coming back to this place, but at the same time I didn't want to look.

The flag on my father's grave was no longer there, but to my relief I saw that several others, though grubby and tattered, were still flying. My father's flag must have blown away in the wind; it had been held down only by a few stones. Otherwise, the grave was exactly as I left it, the inscription and engraving of lilies still pristine on the head-stone. As I climbed the rocky path to stand beside it, I felt hot tears rush up behind my eyes. A group of small boys were watching me from the other side of the cemetery, and I realised that they had been keeping all the graves neat, including my father's. One of them had planted a fresh clod of grass amid the stones on top of the plot, and now he came with a blue plastic watering can and started cleaning the dust from the headstone. They watched, silently, as I lay over the grave and wept. I can be strong anywhere apart from at the grave of my father.

He was a soldier before he became a man. From the age of nine, my father's country was his family, his love and his first priority. But it was his bad luck to be born just as Afghanistan crumbled to dust.

In the same year that he entered the military school system, the Soviet Union invaded Afghanistan. The government and state became puppets of Moscow, up until the mujahideen seized control in 1992, and then the Taliban claimed final victory four years later. There were parts of the military that resisted the creep of Soviet influence and remained loyal to Hafizullah Amin, the deposed president, but they were quickly overwhelmed. The military that my father became a part of was a vassal, embroiled in a conflict fuelled by Cold War rivalry.

My father did not care much for politics: he served under whichever regime was in power. In the Taliban era the army collapsed into a string of warring militias, with little central command. He was lucky that, by then, he had found a role as a teacher at the academy, rather than as a frontline fighter. It saved him from becoming tangled up in the worst events of that era. His reputation in the military far outstripped his rank; almost every talented young soldier joined his classes at some point.

In his last years he served as a commander, training the special operations corps, an elite unit set up in 2011. It was the spearhead in the fight against the Taliban and other extremist groups, and it was highly effective. Perhaps that is part of the reason why he came to accept and support my struggle against them, too. Time after time, throughout his whole life, he put himself in harm's way to defend an idea of Afghanistan.

But although love for his country ran in his blood, he was not cut out to succeed there. He never bribed anyone for favours, nor used his connections to get ahead. He worked his way up honestly, and for that he suffered by stagnation. He saw his students move ahead of him in the ranks, and he never enjoyed material comforts. He never even fully took advantage of the things to which he was entitled. He should have been under twenty-four-hour protection after the attacks on me. But that is not how he wanted to live his life.

On the last day he was alive, he filled in his soldier's diary with orderly, dispassionate precision:

- teach elementary and advanced courses
- repair damaged military radios
- issue warning over night shift reports
- inform those on night shifts that three nights a week, the school commander is on the premises

The last time I saw my dad was at a family gathering in our home in the last days of October 2020. It was only days after the last attack on me. Sitting together, we recited the *hatim*, a prayer that can only be read by those who have memorised the entire Quran. In this prayer you ask God for his forgiveness, and his guidance. It is a special, spiritual prayer for Muslims, more so when we recite it together with our families. After these rituals I always felt a kind of calm, as if all my anger had been quelled. I remember looking at my father's face that afternoon; his eyes were closed and he was swaying slightly as he recited the poetic lines of the prayer. His hair was grey now and his face was lined, but I realised that he looked somehow younger and lighter than he had when I was a child. Maybe it was because he had done his job of raising us, and was now only a few years away from retirement. My mother was looking forward to spending time with him, and having a life in which the two of them could enjoy their marriage without the pressures of his work hanging over them. I wish now that I had looked at him for longer that day. When I close my eyes I can still conjure the outlines of his face and the colour of his eyes, but I struggle to fill in all the lines that creased around the side of his mouth when he smiled, or the exact curve of his forehead.

When we parted, I gave him a brief hug and hurried off. He still had work meetings that day. The security situation in Kabul was worsening, fast. There had been a string of bombings and shootings in recent weeks, including at Kabul University, where twenty-one students were killed by gunmen. A prosecutor from the military courts had been assassinated. My father, like me, had an insight into how grave the situation really was, how quickly the Taliban was gathering power. But we left these things unsaid that day, and I headed back to my office in Maidan Shahr.

The next time I was meant to see him was at a family lunch held on 5 November, to welcome my aunt back to Kabul. She had lived in Germany for more than twenty years, and only came back to visit once a year. She and my mother were close, even after all these years living so far apart, and the return was always a celebration. I had looked forward to it all week, to see my aunt of course but also to catch up properly with my dad. We had both been so busy in recent months that it was rare that we just sat together and laughed. When the day came, I decided to go and pick up the freshest fish that I could find. Before I went to see my family, Bashir, his cousin and I drove with my friend Tamana to Surobi, the place where the Kabul river flows into the Panjshir valley. Forty miles north of the city, the water springs back to life, no longer a polluted trickle but a gushing green snake revived by the melting ice flowing from the mountains. In Surobi there are restaurants lining the river banks where waiters catch fish in front of you and then fry them up on their griddles. There are two special kinds of fish there: small sardines that you can eat in one go, their head and tail and everything, their bones so tender you don't even notice them; and carp so huge they can feed a whole family. There is also everything else in between. Before they slap the fish onto the scorching griddle the chefs season it with masala spices, and then serve it up between bread with salad, to be washed down with cold Fanta or Coke. The area is also famous for its pashmina sellers, who wander the roads with armfuls of scarves made of the softest cashmere. They start by quoting a ridiculous price, which you then haggle down to 300 Afghani (about $4), their real value. When I returned from India I had got out of the practice of haggling, and was ripped off a few times by those pashmina sellers.

There was a time when, if you had asked me what is my favourite place in Afghanistan, I would have told you: Surobi. But its enchanted landscape is now for ever tainted for me by the memory of what happened that day. We were in search of the best fish to take back to Kabul, and Bashir was insisting we drive further. But something made me desperate to turn back. It was an instinct, gnawing inside me.

'Please just turn back to Kabul,' I told Bashir. 'We'll take the fish from the first place.'

Moments later, Bashir's car stuttered to a stop, right in the worst possible place. We had broken down in one of the mobile phone black spots between the mountains, where the signal is patchy at best. That gnawing feeling was deepening. As Bashir and his cousin lifted the bonnet of the car and tried to work out what had happened, I stood on the tips of my toes and waved my phone in the air, trying to find enough signal to send a message. When the bars crept up from one to two, a message flashed through from my dad. A voice message, which he always preferred – he always said he couldn't be bothered tapping away at the screen. I had recently offered to buy him an iPhone, but in his message he was telling me that I didn't have to bother, he had found a different model that he liked and which wasn't nearly as expensive. I smiled as I heard the familiar undulations of his voice, and imagined his confusion at this new technology.

Why would I need an iPhone? he would have thought. *All I want to do is make calls and send messages, I don't need to play games or look at my bank account!*

Before the message had concluded, his voice was cut short by an incoming call. It was Masoom, my driver, and his voice was strained with a panic that I had never heard before.

'Everyone is trying to get hold of you,' he said. 'Your sister Horya just called me. She's crying.'

Thump. I felt my heart hit the bottom of my stomach. I hit my sister's number and she picked up on the first ring. I couldn't make out a word she was saying. It was just howls and sobs down the line, an animal sound that made me shiver.

'Gather yourself!' I told her. 'What has happened?'

'OK, I am telling you, sister,' she said finally, gulping in another huge sob. 'They shot Dad.'

The mountain vista turned to a blur of blues and greens, and sounds seemed to come to me through water.

They shot Dad.

My sister poured out a torrent of details after that, but that line was all I remembered. It replayed in my head as I fumbled in the back seat for my bag. Bashir was by my side now, wanting to know what had happened. I stuttered out the same words.

'They shot Dad.' Then: 'I have to get back to Kabul.'

There was nothing else I could think of. The urge to get to my father's side was as singular as the one that had come over me when I ducked my head down to avoid the assassin's bullet, or took in all the details of the man who was pointing the RPG at me. I knew that in that moment there was nothing more important than being with him. I started trying to flag down cars that were driving in the direction of Kabul, deaf to Bashir's pleas to wait. A black jeep slowed down and pulled up next to me. The driver rolled down his window, thinking that we needed help to restart our car.

'Please,' I begged him. 'My father has been shot and I need to get to him.'

Bashir saw that he could not talk me out of it. Shouting at his cousin to wait with the car, he climbed into the back seat of the jeep. After a few moments' discussion, Tamana got in too. The risk was huge, in retrospect. We were getting into a car with two total strangers, in a place with no mobile phone reception. But the danger didn't even cross my mind. I passed the whole way to Kabul in a mess of emotion, my panic growing the closer we got to the city. Bashir sketched out the few details we knew for the driver of the car. By now I was incapable of doing anything but crying.

'Zarifa, you have to calm yourself,' Tamana told me. 'Call your family. Find out what's happening.'

I tried them all – my mother, my uncles. Nobody was picking up. Finally, my mother's voice came through the speaker. It was strained and hollow, a flat imitation of her usual tone.

'Are you fine?' I asked her, the standard Afghan greeting, which we always start our exchanges with no matter what chaos is unfolding.

'How can I be fine?' she answered. 'I have lost my whole life. They have put three bullets in his head.'

I only found out later how it happened. Thursday was the day my father usually worked late. But on that particular day he was home before my mother. When she returned, she found him standing by the front gate, and he was in the kind of playful mood that had become more usual for him in these recent years.

'Hello, my moon, welcome home!' he shouted, not caring who from the neighbourhood heard him.

My mother scolded him – it is not common for couples to be so publicly affectionate in Afghanistan.

'I don't care what people say,' he told her. 'You are my wife and I enjoy calling you that!'

Inside, he prepared lemon tea and a plate of fruit for her. When some of the fruit fell onto her headscarf he cleaned it off. Then he went into the bathroom and changed out of his army uniform, and into a fresh white shalwar khameez. He lay down on the bed and closed his eyes for a rest. When he woke, he went out to help the neighbours, who were holding a big wedding celebration but did not have anything to play their music on. He took a packet of cinnamon to them so that they could prepare *awang* tea, sent his driver to fetch a new speaker, and set about helping another neighbour mend his water pipe. My dad was like a leader in our neighbourhood: if there were celebrations, he joined them. If there were problems, he fixed them.

That was when the gunmen came. My father was outside, joining two water pipes together, his back turned to his attackers. The car sped through the tight streets of our neighbourhood, slamming to a halt metres away from him. Two armed men jumped out. One pointed his gun at the members of the wedding party, the other used his silenced pistol to shoot my dad three times in the head. Neither of the killers bothered to wear masks, and after they had committed their murder they jumped back in their car and drove into the rush hour. Yet nobody who witnessed the murder could say who they were, or even give a detailed description. Despite the traffic jams, the attackers escaped easily. My brother Roman, only thirteen years old, was standing by our gate and saw everything. My sister Marina, two days away from her sixteenth birthday, came out next. She saw my father lying straight out in the road, his mouth closed, as if he were asleep. It was as if it were a performance, as though someone had laid him out like that.

I grew up with stories of brutal death and desperate flight, of the people who didn't live long enough for me to meet them, brought back to life through tearful reminiscences. I endured my own hardships too, new stories to add to the family album. My upbringing was marred by violence and fear of the people who might mete it out on me. We all have our own ways of dealing with such trauma. For me, my emotional scars have turned into a hard outer shell that might seem unnatural to some, just as the burnt skin on my hands and feet grew back in a new, thickened form. My suffering has made me tougher, more able to fight back tears in situations where even most men would have succumbed. Like many people, I often use humour as my defence, finding black comedy in the most appalling things that have happened to me.

Maybe, to many, I seem cold: an unnatural woman for whom shouting comes easier than tears. In a society where women are expected to be soft and empathetic, naturally maternal figures who move soundlessly through the world, I must look like an abomination. Here's the truth: in Afghanistan it is impossible to be a successful woman without also being an emotionless one. Because here's the nasty trick: although we are expected to feel everything deeply, our emotions are also held against us, and used as the excuse for why we cannot be anything more than a wife and mother. If we cry then we are *hysterical*, they say. If we want to put logic aside to make someone feel better then we are *irrational*. If we feel empathy then we are *weak*.

It is for that reason that, in the life stories that I have recounted so far, you have rarely seen my tears. They came with pain when I was burnt, and they came in anger when my father blocked me from going to school. But my default reaction to trauma is icy detachment, and that too is fodder for my critics. I won't bow to them just to appease them; they do not deserve to see what is really inside me.

But this is the one part of my story that I cannot tell without crying. Every time I speak or even think about my father's murder, my eyes start stinging and within seconds uncontrollable tears are falling down my face. The loss of him has opened up a wound inside me that I cannot feel healing, even with the time that has passed. He was the most important person in my life. You may be thinking: *but he was part of your own pain.* And you would be right. During my childhood our relationship was often fraught, and I know that he did not always do the right thing by me. But the greatest part of this tragedy is that in his last years, he had become the softest, most supportive father I could have wished for. It was as if, after years of trying to impose his ideas on me, he had looked at me one day and realised that he was proud of what I had become.

When he was murdered, I felt a part of my faith in humanity die. In Islam, they say that humans are the pinnacle of all that was created in the universe: the very best thing that God mustered. Yet now, we are seeing how it is humans who are destroying everything. Destroying societies like Afghanistan, with our thirst for power. Destroying nature and other species with our consumerism and greed. Destroying each other with our jealousy and anger. And destroying people like my father, who for all his faults was a good man.

By the time I saw him that day, my father was already in the mortuary of the military hospital. All I wanted to do was to hug him, to hold him and kiss his forehead for the last time. The driver, whose name I never found out and whose face I had already forgotten, drove me to the gate of the hospital and from there I ran through the security checks and corridors. I had a peripheral awareness of my family gathered in the anteroom, and the thick air of grief around them. I ignored them all, and headed for the door. But as I laid my hand on the cold metal handle I came to. For the first time since I had spoken to Horya in the mountains, my mind cleared. Images of him flashed through my head: young and dark-haired when I was a child, a giant of a man looming over me in his uniform, scooping me up and tickling me when he got home from work. Him lying on the floor with me so we could fire marbles at each other, and the pride in his eyes when I got engaged to Bashir. The day he came into my office, grey-haired now but still far taller than me, still the man I looked up to most. I knew that I would find a very different version of my dad on that mortuary slab. And that was not how I wanted to remember him.

It was always my family that I worried about most. It's a trick as old as Afghanistan and as universal as violence: if you can't scare your victim, threaten the people they love. I could withstand any attack against me, and after so many near misses even the thought of death didn't scare me. But I could not bear the grief that was now tearing apart the people I loved most.

My oldest brother Wasil, now twenty-four, was as defenceless as a child again, his beautiful blue-green eyes filled like bottomless lakes with tears. As I turned back from the mortuary door he clung onto my arm.

'Why?' he asked me.

What answer could I give him? I wanted to scream with him but I steeled my emotions. I was aware of my father's brothers and sisters around us. They were crying, too, but I felt no warmth for them. When my father was alive, they would constantly chide him: 'Why did you send your daughter overseas?' Or: 'Why do you let her work as a politician?'

I turned to Wasil and took hold of him.

'He is gone now and we need to behave,' I told him. 'Everyone is here watching. We have a lot of good friends, but also many enemies. They are here to use everything, small and big, against us. We need to be careful. We need to show them that we are the children of this brave man.'

Next I turned to my mother. She was sitting silently in the corner, not crying. Her eyes were not focused on anything, and she twisted a corner of her headscarf in her fingers.

'Take me home, please,' she said, almost inaudibly. When I took her arm and helped her up, I felt how she was shaking to her core. My strong, indomitable mother had endured the death of a father she couldn't even remember. She had maintained her feminine dignity even through one of the most repressive regimes on earth. I had never seen her lose her broad smile for more than a few minutes at a time. But now I saw that there was a piece of her that had been taken for ever the moment the bullets went into my father's head. Her marriage had been arranged when she was still a child and yet she grew to love him with a warmth that broke through the cold rules of marital life in Afghanistan.

Together, we returned home. I had to muster all of my strength to enter the house. The sound of wailing hit us before we had even reached the door. Everyone from our neighbourhood was sitting in the front room. My sisters were there, too, Horya shouting the loudest. She had been especially close to Dad; she always considered herself his favourite.

'I loved him!' she kept shouting at me. 'I loved him more than anyone else.'

'We all loved him,' I replied. 'He was everyone's father.'

Roman, catatonic with shock, had not spoken since it happened. He was walking around, stone-faced and dry-eyed, silently losing his mind. Noman, the youngest, just nine years old, was trying to step up and be the man. He was hugging all his sisters, telling us over and over: 'Don't cry.'

The pull of mass emotion is powerful. Demonstrative grief is a part of Afghan culture, and usually helps us to release our negative emotions in one go, to feel the worst of our pain together so that afterwards we can start healing. But when a wound is so deep, the grief becomes overwhelming rather than therapeutic. My mother, too, was jolted into fierce mourning the moment she stepped into the house. I have spent years encouraging her to let her emotions go more easily, pleading with her to join me in yoga or meditation sessions to release some of the pain built up inside her. She always refused, too set in the Afghan way of stoic suffering to consider reflecting on her feelings. Now, it all spilled out. She was soon so overwrought that she lost consciousness, her mind unable to cope with the loss of the man who had been beside her for twenty-seven years.

It was three in the morning before our house was empty of guests. My mother and I went into her bedroom, and she opened the wardrobe to hug my father's uniforms. They still smelt of his cologne, a musk he had worn every day since I was a child. The jackets held the shape of his shoulders.

'They were not just killing your dad, they were also trying to stop you, and kill you,' she told me.

As I hugged her tight and tried to soothe her, another piece of clothing, wrapped in white cotton and unfamiliar, caught the corner of my eye. The tears gathered again in my mother's eyes as she saw me looking at it.

'That is your wedding dress,' she said. 'Your aunt brought it for you, from Germany. Dad was going to surprise you with it tonight.'

And then my tears came, too.

We hold our funerals the day after death, while the grief is raw and the body of the deceased still holding onto its last flush of life. Although this is the way in our culture and nobody questions it, it always feels too soon. Twenty-four hours earlier my father had been alive, standing at the gate to greet my mother. Now we were to take him out of that gate in a coffin.

We woke early to wash and dress well for the funeral, and to clean the house, just as my father liked. When the undertakers brought his body back for the last time, I remember thinking that it was strange for him to enter without footsteps. Even then, I held out a hope that I might suddenly hear him shout for me, or burst through the door and tell us it had all been a cruel practical joke. But when I looked at his body, my hopes died. He was still so handsome, but his right eye was slightly open, and above it there was a gaping hole, red around the edges where his blood had spilled out. I wanted to sit there with him for hours, savouring every last moment to look upon him. When they came to take him away I begged them not to. I couldn't bear the finality.

We closed the lid of his coffin, and I placed the flag of Afghanistan over the top. As I laid the red, green and black cloth over my father, I promised him that I would take care of the family, and make sure that nothing bad happened to the people he loved. He had suffered enough and now he shouldn't worry any more. He should rest in peace.

The funeral was full of my father's friends and colleagues, people whose respect he had earned during thirty-seven years of military service: a lifetime. There should have been officials from the defence ministry there, too, given his rank of colonel and long service. There were none. I was furious at the whole apparatus of the country. I held every official who had refused to take my concerns seriously responsible for my dad's death. After the second attack against me they had given me an old bulletproof car, which was always breaking down and constantly had to be taken to the mechanics. After the third attack they gave me two bodyguards, but without weapons. I went out and found Kalashnikovs for them myself. They were always one step behind, reacting to the last thing that had happened rather than planning ahead.

I went to visit his grave alone in the late afternoon on the day of his funeral. I did it secretly; police officers had been guarding my family home in case the killers came back for more blood. At last, they were taking the threat seriously, when already it was too late. Hours after my father's murder, the police upped my bodyguard team from two to five. Bashir took to going around the neighbourhood with his gun, on the lookout for anyone suspicious. We simply didn't trust the police to do their jobs properly. The day after my father's funeral we went to the mosque in Makroyan to say prayers for the safety of his soul. Then my work as the new head of the family began.

I knew that first I had to move everyone to a new house – they would not be safe as long as they stayed where they were. It took them a few days to build up the courage to step outside the door. I was terrified, too, that another attack was coming. I tried to keep my fears hidden, but within weeks of my father's death I was again receiving warnings from the national directorate of security. This time, they had found out that the Taliban planned to kill me as I made my weekly visit to my father's grave.

My father's murder changed me. I had prided myself on staying in my post in Wardak even when most people there wanted me gone; I saw my stubbornness as my best trait. Now, I knew that I had to put myself and my family first. When I was the one under attack, I found it easy to laugh away the danger, batting away others' concerns with a single word and a flick of my hand. I thought that my work came before everything, and that if I died while doing it then so be it. I would be a martyr, and my death would highlight the outrages that Afghan women were having to deal with, daily. Whenever I felt the first stabs of fear in my stomach, I turned them instead into anger. I did that by examining the reasons why such things were happening to me, and to my country. Why did people want to attack me? Because I have a voice. Why don't people want women to have a voice? Because they are scared that Afghanistan will change, that the balance of power will tip and never go back. They attack me because I am committed to my cause, and know that I will never stop speaking against them. They attack me because I am strong.

What has hurt most, was that even when I was so horrifically burned in the first attack, there were still people spreading gossip about me, saying that I had caused the accident because I was drunk – a total lie. After the subsequent attacks and my father's murder, others wrote on social media that I had orchestrated the attack because I wanted political asylum in the US. If that had ever been my aim, I would not have needed to sear the skin from my feet and hands and scar myself for ever to achieve it. When I travelled to Washington, DC, to collect my award from the state department I was given a multiple-entry visa. While I was there, I showed many people the threats that I had received.

'When you come home, we will see you,' one faceless, nameless correspondent threatened me.

'We know you perfectly. We know your home address,' wrote another. 'We know your siblings. We know what schools they attend, and when they go to class. We know how they get there and back. We know everything about you, too.'

My friends in the US tried to persuade me to stay for a month, at least, to let the danger simmer down. I refused. So what was this cheap slander, to claim that I was trying to win sympathy to get a new life in America? I had been travelling all over the world since I went to India a decade earlier, and on numerous occasions I had been offered opportunities to begin afresh, away from Afghanistan. I always refused, for one reason: my motivation to get out of bed each morning, out of a hospital bed or a rolled-out mattress on the floor of an office, was to improve my country.

Every time I travelled back and forth between Kabul and Maidan Shahr I used a different car – Bashir's old Ford, the bullet holes patched up, a friend's car, or taxis, none of them armoured but the subterfuge was its own kind of defence. By now I knew that my enemies' most dangerous weapon was intelligence. The Taliban had almost encircled Maidan Shahr with the villages they now controlled, and from there they could easily reach into the city with their networks. It had occurred to me that they might even be paying off the people who watched security cameras on the highway, or the police or the army. Although I hated to think of it, there was also the possibility that they might have spies within the municipality itself. I knew at the very least that there were people inside the compound who despised me. One Thursday lunchtime, I went to the bank in the centre of Maidan Shahr, where the municipality kept its account. After all the attacks, I now had to use a car even for short trips. When I returned half an hour later, the guard at the gate stopped us, and refused to lift the barrier. He was relatively new on the job, but he certainly knew who I was.

'Where are you going?' he asked, abruptly.

'Back to the office,' I replied. 'I'm the mayor.'

One of the officers from the revenue team was with me – a Hekmatyar man, who over the months I had been in office had proved himself to be honest and loyal. He was enraged by this guard's impertinence, and he got out of the car and walked up to him.

'We went out of this gate just thirty minutes ago.'

The guard still wouldn't budge: 'No, you're not allowed in.'

Now I got out of the car, too. I was one of the two most powerful people working in this compound, and did not want to leave my staff to fight my battles.

'I'm the mayor,' I repeated. 'How do you not know me? But who are you? I've never seen you here.'

Then it happened, in slow motion as if a nightmare. The guard lifted his gun and cocked it, pointing it straight at my head.

'Go away or I'll shoot you!'

The revenue officer ushered me away as the guard went crazy, kicking my car and hitting it with the butt of his gun.

I complained to everyone – to the governor, and the national directorate of security, whose uniform that guard was wearing. How had he managed to pass through their vetting process?

The next day he was no longer there. I never saw him again. But I wanted a full investigation. I had showed the guard my identity and security cards, yet still he had pointed his gun at me. That meant that he was ready to kill me, even though – or perhaps because – he knew who I was. I was told he was simply transferred to a new post in another district. Later I heard that he had killed one of his colleagues, and then that he had defected to the Taliban.

Each time I set off for Kabul, I let it be known within the office that I was going out on a short trip within the city and would be back within a couple of hours. I would never head straight for the highway. First, we would do a detour to the radio station, or to see the chief of police. Instead of my headscarf I would wear a turban, so that through the smoked glass of the car window I looked like a man. The one thing I never agreed to do to hide my identity was wear a burka. I was fighting for women to have the right to step out onto the streets without one in places like Wardak, and so to wear one, even if it was for my safety, would have undermined all of my work. A burka would have felt like a cage.

Throughout the spring of 2021, the Taliban inched closer to Maidan Shahr. The Jaghatu district, a place of gentle green hills and ancient ruins, was one of the first parts of Wardak to fall completely to the Taliban. The militants had killed Raz Mohammed Waziri, Jaghatu's governor, in October 2019; after that, the fighting there never ceased. Taliban fighters from other areas poured into Jaghatu, overwhelming the demoralised security forces, and capturing an old fort, which they turned into their HQ. From there, they immediately started imposing their own social order; they planted roadside bombs that had to be swept for every morning in areas still just barely controlled by the army, and banned women from leaving their houses unaccompanied. From Maidan Shahr, it was clear that the Taliban was winning, getting stronger every day. The army was running out of food and weapons. Yet the officials sitting in the defence ministry in Kabul issued near-daily press releases about the areas the army had recaptured, framing it as if they were winning the war.

In May 2021, fifteen days into a major battle in Jaghatu, Wardak's chief of police called the provincial governor, begging for air support and weapons. He said they could not hold out much longer without a resupply. Jaghatu is twenty miles from Kabul, yet no back-up was sent. I could not understand why; I too was making constant calls to my contacts in the defence ministry and the national directorate of security. Finally, they said they would send a helicopter; however, they said they would touch down on a spot controlled by the Taliban. I told officials at the ministry as much; so did the governor and the chief of police. Yet that was where the helicopter landed, only to be attacked and destroyed minutes later. When a team of special forces commandos was eventually sent to Jaghatu, they stayed only for two days. The area fell entirely to the Taliban. That scenario was just one of many playing out in countless other districts, right across Afghanistan.

Almost half the entire province was outside government control, and by now the road to Kabul was so dangerous that I stayed mostly in my office. Every night, from midnight until break of dawn, I heard bullets whistling through the air past my window. Most nights, the fighting would come so close that a staff member would knock on my door and tell me not to sleep, in case we had to flee. On the days when the fighting in the villages was intense, I would head secretly to the radio station just before sundown and spend the night there instead. When the sun rose a kind of normality would return to the city. The shopkeepers would open their businesses and the cleaners would sweep bullet casings from the streets. In the bazaar the small talk centred around who had been involved in the fights the night before, who had been injured, or killed. It was certain that some of the people walking around

Maidan Shahr like normal citizens in the daytime were returning after dark with Kalashnikovs. As time went on, some grew so bold as to flaunt their affiliation. One day, a member of the municipality revenue team was shooed away by a shopkeeper who boasted that he was a member of the Taliban, and that there would be consequences if he kept being hassled to pay his rates.

When I was offered a transfer to a new post at the defence ministry in Kabul, I accepted. There was no way I could keep telling my mother that all would be fine, when there was no safe way for me to continue working in Maidan Shahr. Every time I came back to Kabul for the night, I went to my family's home instead of my own apartment, as much to show them that I was OK as for their company. Every time I left them it was more of a wrench. I could see the trauma of my dad's death etched into each of their faces. I couldn't bear to think what it would do to them if I were taken from them, too. If I were killed, how could I fulfil my promises to my family? I was being targeted because of the work I was doing in service of my country and people. But I was also a daughter and sister. I was respected, by some, for my profession, but I was loved by my family for who I am. Filling both of those roles was harder than I ever imagined it could be. I felt pulled in opposite directions, but really I had only one choice: my family had to come first.

I was happy, at least, with the legacy I had left for my successor. Two and a half years into my tenure, I had the office functioning as I wanted it. I had taken on five young women as interns, and the city was cleaner and brighter than it had ever been. We had planted green verges and created pedestrian areas where people could walk for enjoyment. As well as renewing the team and sorting out the revenue, I had made sure that all the systems and records were digitised, as they would have been in any modern municipality. There had been four different governors in Wardak in the time that I had been mayor: I had survived in the job far longer than anyone had expected, and pushed my luck far enough. In the defence ministry, I would be able to do my job, and see my friends and family. I would also be working for the department my dad had devoted his life to, working among his students, colleagues and friends. I felt it would bring me closer to him.

Still, on the day my transfer was officially announced, I felt a gut pull towards Maidan Shahr. I had never expected to live in Wardak, let alone take up a job there. When I left my cousin Qabila to move back to Kabul in 2001, I felt so relieved that I did not have to spend my whole life in this restrictive place. If Bashir had not convinced me that it was the right place to set up a radio station, I might never have returned to Wardak. But something here had grabbed hold of me. Scratching beneath its harsh exterior, first with my radio recorder and then as mayor, I had discovered a place full of good people who needed an honest system to let them shine. There were plenty here who did not support the Taliban, and even those who did often had their reasons – lack of education, a promise of paradise, a thirst for revenge. Those problems could be tackled with good leadership. But good leaders are my country's rare commodity.

As I entered my office for the last time, I found the

entire staff of the municipality waiting for me, not only the bureaucratic staff, but also the gardeners and street cleaners. Outside, there were still demonstrations against me – they had never given up the whole time I had been in office – but within the compound I had managed to earn respect. Even Lawang Faizan, the new governor and a member of Hekmatyar's party, was sorry to see me go. The women who worked in the municipality and governorate had written goodbye letters to me, and one of them presented me with a beautifully decorated cake.

'You came here clean and you are leaving clean,' one of the letters read. 'All the corrupt leaders should learn from you.'

That night, I stayed at the radio station for the last time. It was the fiercest night of fighting I ever experienced in Maidan Shahr. The bullets were flying into our compound, and elsewhere in the city a rocket slammed into the local branch of the directorate of information. Somehow, it seemed a fitting end.

'Look!' one of my bodyguards laughed, and then addressed me with an honorific denoting respect. '*Ghafari Sahib*; you've been appointed somewhere else but you're still here, so maybe tonight you will die here.'

Eight

The first refugees arrived in Kabul as the snow melted on the mountaintops in the spring of 2021, a slow trickle of cars piled with mattresses and suitcases. These early arrivals were absorbed into the homes of their city-dwelling relatives, and it was only when the poorer influx came – the women with their children, their husbands missing – that Kabulis could no longer close their eyes to what was happening beyond the city limits. The parks started filling up with tents, some of them proper structures, some just tarpaulin stretched among the trees. In the daytime, the women sat on scrappy rugs laid out on the grass, blank-eyed and silent.

In my new posting at the defence ministry in Kabul, my job was to take care of the families of soldiers who had been killed or disabled in action, or were prisoners of war. There were many of them. According to estimates, there were some 2.5 million widows in Afghanistan whose husbands were killed in one or other of the country's conflicts. I was always pained to see the number of women begging on the streets of Kabul, most of them forced to do so because their husband was dead and they had no other means of making money. If they had been allowed an education, they might have had some saleable skills. The widows of soldiers and government workers were, at least, entitled to a small pension. If their husband had been a normal soldier, they would continue to receive his full salary. Their children also received extra benefits until the girls were married and the boys turned eighteen. If the soldier had been a colonel, like my father, they were promoted to the rank of general after their death.

Now, the Taliban's sweep across the country was creating a new generation of widows. What's more, many of them feared that the Taliban would also punish them for the fact that their dead husbands had worked for the national army. The women gathered what they could and fled their villages for the capital, which they believed to be a beacon of safety.

I went out into the park on Shahr-e Naw to speak to the women, and find out which of them would be entitled to aid from the defence ministry. Children flocked around me and gripped onto my hands as soon as I got out of the car. The park was so filled with tents that there were hardly any empty patches of grass left.

'Who here is the wife of a soldier?' I shouted.

Immediately, a line of women started forming around me. Some had lost only their husbands, others their sons too. They were bereaved, penniless and terrified. Their families and their homes had been stolen from them, and all I could offer was a meagre payment from the government. Yet I presented a small ray of hope in this bleak situation.

'What will I do?' one woman asked me. 'I have nothing, no job and no home.'

'The Taliban came into our village,' another said. 'We hardly had time to collect anything, we just ran.'

For an hour, I listened to story after story, taking down the women's details to enter onto my database at the defence ministry. I handed out my personal number too, telling the women to call me if they needed anything. But even as I said it, I wondered how long I would be able to keep helping them, or even working for my country. Behind the scenes the government was crumbling, and with it the country. By the time I returned to the car, I was crying too, and one of the women dried my face with her headscarf.

In the back of our minds we all knew that Kabul was not Afghanistan – it was our New York to the USA, our Paris to France, our London to the UK. A half-hour drive out of the city took you to the villages where the Taliban governed and social codes had not changed since the nineties. If anything, support for the Taliban grew stronger in these places after 2001, galvanised by the American airstrikes that always killed more civilians than fighters. After the Doha Agreement was signed between the US and the Taliban in February 2020, promising an end to war and American troop withdrawal, the fighting only intensified and the body count soared – on all sides. Death was no leveller in Afghanistan. In places where battles raged, usually the poorest, most conservative villages, Taliban-supporting mullahs told their congregations that the men serving in the national army were not Muslims. The bodies of slain soldiers were often left on the battlefield, their underequipped comrades unable or unwilling, or too scared of retribution, to collect them. As the violence soared, Afghanistan splintered again, into provinces, tribes and villages. A dead soldier, if not a son of a particular area of battle, might as well have come from the moon. Afghans were strangers to each other.

The bodies of men who died fighting for the Taliban, on the other hand, were brought back to their villages with great ceremony, welcomed home by everyone, and given a distinguished funeral. The mullahs would often present the family with a certificate, confirming that their dead son had gone to heaven as a reward for carrying out jihad. They believed that, in heaven, they would be greeted by seventy-two virgins, their reward for the abstinence they had endured in life. In turn, such a show impressed the younger boys who were coming of age, prompting them to think about following the same path. Certainly better to end up in heaven and surrounded by available women, they thought, than rot away in the corner of a field.

The balance between progress in the cities and regression in the villages was delicate, and as soon as the US began negotiating with the Taliban it started tipping in the latter's favour. The Kabul we had come to love was a mirage, yet we had fooled ourselves into believing it was real.

My position and department were brand new, created by presidential decree. I was to take all the information on war widows, disabled soldiers and prisoners of war from around the country, and ensure that the existing systems were working properly. By the time I started my job the money was still not being handed out consistently. Four years earlier there had been a huge scandal, when it was revealed that military widows were being forced to give sexual favours to officials to receive the money owed to them. Or if a widow had a connection with someone in government or with a powerful warlord, she was able to access her pension. But for those without connections – most of them – it was almost impossible.

I was also tasked with liaising with the generals to ensure that the information I was receiving was correct. Part of the Doha Agreement stipulated that, before peace talks could begin, there would be a prisoner exchange: 5,000 Taliban members would be released from government prisons, in return for 1,000 Afghan national army soldiers being held by the Taliban. The exchange was completed in September 2020, but with the scrappy record-keeping in the ministry we had no way of knowing for sure who had been released, and which wives needed to keep receiving benefits for their incarcerated husbands. It was a fundamental job, vital to the functioning of my office. Yet every time I approached the generals for information, they shooed me away. When I complained to my bosses in the ministry, they sighed and told me this was a perennial problem. The defence ministry was split into military and civilian parts, and the former liked to lord it over the latter, even though we were all working for the same team. The generals thought they were showing their strength. I couldn't believe how weak they all seemed.

*

Often, the biggest problem a war widow faced was the family of her dead husband, whose parents often intervened to try to claim the benefits for themselves. Soldiers sometimes signed documents while they were alive expressly stating who their salary should go to if they were killed in action, and this should have been the end of the matter. But there were many cases where the document was disputed, with families claiming that it had been faked. Some faked the document themselves, claiming to be the beneficiaries. I had many women come to me, begging for my help, telling me of their fathers-in-law who were trying to take custody of their children and throw them out of the family house, as if their expiry date had passed with their husbands' death. We sent such cases to the courts, which rarely did anything about them. Either the case would languish in a waiting list, or if it did come before the judges, who were usually men, they would rule against the woman. In the meantime, she had few means to support herself and her children.

One woman came to my office with an old man. I could sense the hostility between them. They had never met until the man who linked the two of them was killed. The man's son had left home as a teenager and travelled to Kabul to join the army. There, he had met the woman and married her. As they built their life together, his mother died and his father remarried. He had no further relationship with his father or step-siblings. Yet the father resurfaced when he heard about his son's death. He argued that he should be getting his son's salary, not this woman he had never heard of. The wife, meanwhile, had no way of knowing if this man really was her late husband's father or an imposter trying his luck. She had three children to take care of, and was pregnant with a fourth. I decided to send the case to the justice ministry, but to placate them in the meanwhile I gave them both the salary, divided equally between them. After two days they were back in the office. This time, the woman had come with all her children, the oldest not quite six years old. The alleged father-in-law had brought a younger man with him, and was now lobbying for all of the money, not half.

As a woman, I could see what the men were doing. They were trying to use all their body language to intimidate and diminish the widow and walk away with money that was owed to her. The younger guy slouched in a chair in my office, spreading his legs wide to take up as much space as possible while he shouted into his phone with infuriating nonchalance.

'Yeah, we're at the defence ministry. Don't worry, we're going to sort it,' he said.

I snapped. 'Turn off your phone and sit properly!' I shouted.

His head flicked upwards, amazement in his eyes. I don't think anyone had corrected his behaviour before.

'This is not a kindergarten,' I continued. 'Behave. Tell me who you are.'

'I'm his nephew,' he said, sheepishly.

'Then you're nobody in this conflict. Sit there properly and stay silent.'

The old man made his case for why he deserved all the money, his logic being that the son wouldn't even have existed without him. Though the dead soldier had officially filed the paperwork before he was killed, naming his wife as his beneficiary – a cut-and-dried case – Afghanistan's social codes meant that I could not simply tell the old man to his face that he was wrong.

The woman was crying.

'Whatever is his right is OK with me,' she said. 'But I don't know him. Please also give me enough to survive and to look after my children and this baby in my belly.'

The old man snorted. 'How can you prove that this is my son's child?'

To say such a thing to a woman was beyond disrespect. I could see so clearly what was happening. This man had never been there for his son while he was alive, nor done anything to help his grandchildren. But as soon as there were benefits to be had he was there, claiming what he believed was his blood-right. I was simmering with rage but took a breath, pushed down my anger, and addressed him in an even tone.

'Actually, according to the law she should be getting everything,' I told him. 'I will be sending all the money to her account. Whatever else you want to do, you can do outside my office. But if anything happens to this woman, we will know the reason.'

Remaining calm in such situations was always the hardest part of my job, both in the defence ministry and as mayor. In Maidan Shahr, people would call me an unbeliever or a whore, and I simply had to tolerate it. Afghanistan's social codes meant that I had to preface everything I said to this man with assurances that I respected him, his age and his feelings, even though he had shown none of the same respect to me or to this blameless woman.

Another day, as I sat in my office, I heard a desperate shouting from the corridor. It was a woman, crying and refusing to leave, despite the best efforts of other officers. My assistant told me that she came often, always shouting and causing a scene.

'Why doesn't anyone listen to her?' I asked.

I went out, took the woman's hand and led her into my office. When I had settled her into a chair, I shut the door and told her to gather herself.

'It's just us, and I am listening to you with fresh ears,' I said. 'Tell me. What is your problem?'

The woman, it turned out, was looking for her son, whom she had not heard from in more than four years. He was a soldier, and his posting had been changed. But almost as soon as he had moved, he had stopped calling. Time and again she had gone to the army to ask what had happened to him. First, she was told that he had deserted. Then, she was told he had been killed in action. A third official told her that he had been taken prisoner by the Taliban. She had brought an armful of documents with her, backing up everything she was telling me: three letters stamped with the seal of the Afghan government, giving three different versions of events. Her mother's instinct told her that her son was dead, but in order to fully believe it she needed to see his grave. She wanted his body returned to her so that she could give him a proper burial and start to grieve. She was also entitled to receive his salary – four years' worth of payments that had just disappeared in a mess of bureaucracy. I could not do anything about finding her son's body, but I could lobby for restitution of money owed to her. In the end, I managed to get her two years of backdated payments and the promise of a piece of land.

*

I never received a single paycheque from the ministry of defence. I wasn't alone – nobody working there was paid for months in 2021. We were told that it was because the payment systems were being digitised, but looking back it was a sign of how rapidly things in Afghanistan were unravelling. All my savings had drained away. When I had been mayor of Wardak, my salary was not huge but it was enough to keep my family afloat. They were still not getting what they were owed from my father's pension. Now, I had nothing left to give them, nor could I pay my own bills. In desperation, I contacted one of my father's friends, a doctor in the military hospital. He agreed to lend me US$3,000 – money I wondered how I would ever repay.

Our soldiers were also suffering from a backlog of unpaid salaries, even as they were fighting increasingly desperate battles against the Taliban. I received messages via my Facebook account from soldiers stationed all over the country, many of whom had not been paid in months. It did not matter so much for them while they were on duty, out in the field, but it was a matter of survival for their families, who were without any income. Half their mind was on the fight in front of them, the other half at home. No wonder they were losing.

'We're trapped between battles,' read one note. 'We're under attack and are not receiving support.'

Another: 'It's been more than six months. I want a few days' leave to see my family but they are not allowing me.'

And at the same time, I was receiving yet more messages from widows who were not receiving what they were owed.

'I have not received my husband's salary since his death.'

'I have not received my piece of land.'

Soon, under the weight of these complaints, I realised this was not just about mismanagement: this was a system failure, unfolding right in front of me.

The chaos started at the top, as it always does. Asadullah Khalid, the defence minister, had been forced into a long leave of absence due to poor health, and was eventually replaced by a caretaker, Bismillah Khan Mohammadi, in June 2021. By then, the situation had become critical. The US had begun its withdrawal a month earlier, and the Taliban were now waging fierce offensives in all but six of Afghanistan's thirty-four provinces. The Afghan security forces, increasingly on their own, were still entirely dependent on funding from the US, NATO and the UN, which meant that every small decision within the defence ministry needed the approval of the US generals in charge of operations in Afghanistan. It was the US who insisted that the ministry digitise its systems, a distraction from more pressing issues. We had far bigger and more urgent problems to deal with. We were at war, yet hamstrung. The Taliban boasted of protecting the US troops as they withdrew, and turned their guns on their own country-men. I knew there were Afghan soldiers fighting in the countryside who were drinking their own urine because they had run out of water and whose families were calling them, telling them they did not have enough money to eat. These soldiers, who were not being paid and saw their country slipping out of their control, lost morale, and the will to fight.

In April 2021 we had a visit from Antony Blinken,

US Secretary of State in newly elected President Biden's administration. I was one of the officials invited to the US embassy to meet with him, to convey the perspective of Afghan women. I knew this might be my last chance to lobby the US before the country fell entirely to the Taliban. This time, I did not bother with diplomacy or politeness. The deal with the Taliban and the decision to withdraw troops might have been made in Trump's chaotic White House, but it was clear that Biden thought it right to continue with the plan. I told Blinken that this was a terrible mistake, one that gave the extremists a huge platform and boost to their morale. I told him that as Afghan women we would be paying the price, as we had done with the fall of every regime since the Shah. I told him how I was getting reports from all over the country about the conditions our soldiers were fighting in, and how many were dying – hundreds each day. I implored him not to make any more strategic mistakes. I also wanted to know what the US was doing to put pressure on Pakistan. Everyone knew that Taliban leaders were travelling through there to reach Doha, the Qatari capital where the talks with the US had taken place. It was public knowledge that Taliban leaders had been holding meetings with the head of the Pakistan army.

Blinken replied to my questions with a few sentences, delivered with an easy confidence that betrayed his total misunderstanding of this unfolding catastrophe.

'We have control over everything. We will ensure that nothing is ruined,' he said. 'If the Taliban does not obey or follow their promises in regards to women's education, we will not support their government.'

Then I understood. The US was entirely willing to let the Taliban have Afghanistan. Any talk of a peace deal, or of a power-sharing government, was just sweet words to cover up what this really was: a defeat. America was abandoning my country, exactly twenty years after it had arrived with its bombs and promises of democracy.

Maidan Shahr fell to the Taliban on 14 August 2021, two months after I had moved to the defence ministry. Three days before it fell, General Abdul Satar Mirzakwal, then interior minister, had been telling journalists of the government's plan to prevent the Taliban from advancing further, by recruiting local leaders to form security cordons around the cities. There were plenty of volunteers; however, they suffered the same problems that haunted the army. The government could not provide them with enough weapons or supplies. The nightly fighting reached a crescendo, until the last resistance broke. The governor fled, and the victorious Taliban fighters moved into his office with barely a shot fired. The Taliban, high on their victory, started reorganising Wardak to their liking, appointing their own people to the offices in Maidan Shahr that I had worked so hard to reform. It was they who appointed the new mayor of Wardak.

Within hours, a Taliban leader in Wardak paid a visit to a relative to ask about me, and my location. He said the Taliban knew that I was working at the defence ministry, and that they would find me, and Bashir, too. I knew he was telling the truth. It was impossible to hide from an adversary that hid itself in plain sight. If there was a place in Afghanistan where I could have escaped from them, I would have gone. No such place existed.

For twenty years the US and the Afghan government had brashly claimed they were winning, holding up their control of Kabul as evidence that they reigned over the whole country. But even as the Taliban had disappeared from the capital it seeped into the fabric of Afghanistan, until it became part of its very chemistry.

The same day that Maidan Shahr fell, so too did Jalalabad, which sits at the main border crossing between Afghanistan and Pakistan. Its capture cut off a major life-line for those hoping to escape. The capital was encircled. The Western diplomats and the Afghan politicians in whom they had invested so many billions started to plan their escape.

Kabul was still Kabul, right to the end. A month before the Taliban rode into the city I sat with my sisters, my youngest brother Noman and my cousin in one of those fashionable new cafés. We had been shopping: the Eid festival was fast approaching, when everyone buys new clothes and gifts for each other and each family slaughters a sheep to share with the poor. Weighed down by bags and exhausted from walking all afternoon, we flopped into comfy velvet chairs and exhaled, ordering hot chocolates and laughing at the jokes we had been sharing throughout the day. Soon our conversation turned to the latest news from the provinces. The Taliban was moving towards us, an advancing mob crossing deserts and mountain passes. Yet it felt theoretical, like something in a movie or a computer game. As I looked around at the fashionable girls in that café, who had never known anything but this Kabul, my laughter fizzled out. I realised they had no idea what was closing in on us.

'What do you think it would look like if the Taliban came into Kabul?' I asked Horya, my eldest sister. 'How would you feel?'

'I feel like I might stop laughing if it happened,' she said, still laughing nonetheless.

I turned to Sorya and asked her the same question. She was born a year after the Americans came, but seemed to carry an inherited memory of the Taliban in her bones.

'There would be no university, no life, no job, nothing,' she said. 'I feel it would be better to die than to live that life.'

Marina was the youngest, but her reaction was the most visceral: 'I would jump out the window of our apartment.' Then she shook herself, and started laughing, too. 'Imagine, if they were really here!' she said. 'Taliban fighters sitting at this very table and drinking coffee.'

Like that, it had turned from a political discussion about a very possible near future to a story of make-believe. That's what denial does to you, and what Kabul can do, too. It is a ridiculous way to think, because nothing is for ever in that city. Already, in my lifetime, it had changed hands three times, from mujahideen to Taliban to US-backed government. Expecting that it would never change again was as foolhardy as believing that a bubble would never burst: it always does, in the end.

On the day the Taliban came, I pulled on my high heels at the front door of my mother's apartment.

'You can't be going to work today!' she exclaimed when she saw me.

It was 7.30 on the morning of 15 August 2021, a Saturday, and the second day of the working week in Afghanistan. I was heading to my office in the defence ministry. But my mother had spotted some posts on Facebook.

'Maybe the Taliban are coming to Kabul today,' she said, and I saw a spark of fear in her dark eyes.

Recently, I had stopped looking at social media. I made an effort to avoid the news. The previous night, I had curled up with my little brother in front of a cheesy Bollywood film, pretending all was normal, for my sake more than his.

'Don't believe everything you read on Facebook!' I told her. 'Don't worry, of course they're not in Kabul.'

I believed my own words, despite everything I knew. They couldn't be in the city – not this quickly. The village boys with their Kalashnikovs had swept through the provinces easily enough, through the conservative places where their support is rock solid. But Kabul, the energetic, modern capital? *No way*, I thought, *not here*.

My mother trusted me. 'We're out of oil and flour,' she said, abandoning her attempt to keep me at home. 'Bring me back some money today.'

I hoped I could return that evening with a purse full of Afghanis, hand a bundle over to my mother and tell her to buy as much as she needed. That was what I was thinking about as I closed the front door. But I knew my bank account would probably be empty.

'Let's go to the nearest bank,' I told my driver as I climbed into the back seat of my car. It was more than a half-hour drive to downtown Kabul, a route churning with traffic and checkpoints. The city slid by my window, the low-rise honey-coloured apartment blocks sharpening into glass and steel. But we soon stuttered to a halt. The traffic was worse than terrible; it was immobile. Hundreds of cars choked the boulevards. An hour later and we were still six blocks from the banks, but I couldn't bear to sit there any longer.

'Wait here, I'll walk!' I said.

'It's not safe for you to go alone,' my bodyguard told me. These days, he went with me everywhere.

Together we walked to Shahr-e Naw, Kabul's fanciest end. I peered into the windows of the boutiques. All of them were closing up. The other people on the pavement were rushing, worry etched on their brows.

Something big is happening, I thought, and pulled my phone from my handbag. *Maybe it's about the people who've been displaced.*

I snapped some pictures and shot some videos of the panicked people rushing along the pavements. Kabulis needed to see the desperation of their countrymen. They needed to realise how fortunate they were, in comparison.

'What are you doing?' a man shouted at me as I circled around with my phone. 'This isn't the time for selfies! Protect yourself. Go home!'

My bank account said zero, as I expected. I would disappoint my mother but at least I had tried. The driver and I returned to the car, and set off for the defence ministry. It was another infuriating journey through unyielding traffic, starting and then stopping ten seconds later. When we arrived at the ministry the atmosphere there was strange too. There was a cash point in the foyer, and a crowd had congregated around it. Everyone was there, from the top officials to the tea boy. Everywhere else, the building echoed hollowly. There was only one guard at the gate, instead of the usual friendly trio who gave me a respectful greeting every morning and a warm goodbye each afternoon. In the deserted corridors, I sensed a dangerous static.

I took the lift up to my office, a small room on the fourth floor. I placed my bag on my desk and reached for my phone to start checking what on earth was happening. Before I could even unlock it, a soldier was tapping lightly on the open door.

'Ma'am,' he said, 'all female staff are ordered to leave. The Taliban are in the middle of the city and could come here any time. You have to go.'

First my mother and now this guy? I was in denial, I now realise. I didn't even believe what my own colleagues were telling me.

I need to hear this from the top, I thought. I put my bag on my desk and clutched my phone, pushing past the soldier. *The minister will tell me what's happening.*

In the corridors I shouted out to everyone I passed, increasingly frantic, desperate for just one of them to say this was all a joke. None of them did.

'Just go home,' said one of the deputy minister's personal assistants, already in his jacket and making his way towards the stairs. 'They're coming. They are taking everything. We're done here.'

Home? I nearly laughed out loud at the idea, and at

226

the same time felt fear rising in my stomach. The Taliban knew me well, and for certain they knew where I lived. Maybe they would be coming to the ministries first, but at least we had strength in numbers here. Our soldiers would be able to fight back. When they went to my home – and they would – there would be nobody to protect me and my family. And then, I felt disgust. Why were we giving up this easily? Why was our legitimate government surrendering without even the smallest struggle?

'Go home,' another assistant told me. Those words were turning into a bad mantra. Practicalities started flooding my brain. I would have to find my family a new safehouse, if such a place even existed any more. I didn't have the money to pay for a car and driver to take them there, and I could hardly expect the driver hired for me by the ministry to abandon his own family to help us. Where would we go? How would we survive? As I came to the door of the minister's office one of his assistants stopped me.

'Go home,' he said. 'Protect yourself.'

But by now I couldn't stop myself. I entered the office and found the minister talking on the phone. He turned to me and spoke before I'd even said anything.

'You'll be given money,' he told me. 'Just wait there, take the money and then go.'

Those were the words that broke my heart. I did not care about the money.

Back in the assistant's office I heard rumours flying around me. A plane had landed at the presidential palace, someone said. President Ghani was preparing to flee.

Worries began gathering in my mind: home, family, Bashir, nation. Someone pushed 30,000 Afghanis into my hand, a bundle of scrappy notes, and only a fraction of what I was owed.

I was not there for money, but at that moment something inside of me broke. 'I want my four months' salary!' I shouted.

I knew even as I said it that it was a ridiculous request, my last flourish as the difficult woman who refused to back down. The second after the words left my mouth I turned and ran back to my office. Inside, I snatched my bag from the desk. How I wish now that I'd taken a minute to gather a few of my things. Even a last proper look at them would have been something I could hold onto, a comforting memory that might have cushioned the bleak reality that followed. The framed print of the national anthem. The photos of the president and of my father, the Afghan flag I had hung behind my chair. Photographs and letters, the mementos of my career arranged in the cabinet. I wonder what happened to all those things. I wonder who is sitting at my desk now.

In the half hour since I had arrived at the defence ministry, the surrounding streets had turned into a desperate carnival. The roads were blocked with cars, all the drivers leaning on their horns in a continuous, insistent blare. On the pavements, the people moved in a half-run, their eyes fixed ahead, their thoughts somewhere else. My driver had already left, and it would take him too long to fight his way back. No taxi would stop for me. I started walking in the direction of my mother's house.

I realised when my phone started buzzing again that I was still clutching it in my fist.

'Your sisters are not at home!' my mother cried.

Both of them were university students, and had left home that morning in their college girl outfits: jeans and headscarves with bags full of books. Horya was in the second year of a civil engineering degree; Sorya in the first year of political science.

I called Sorya first.

'Don't worry, I'm nearly home,' she said. If she was scared, her voice did not let on.

I dialled Horya. No answer. Again and again I pressed the green call button, letting it ring until the recorded message came on. I felt panic rising from my gut up into my throat. Again, I pressed call. No answer. I had to get a taxi now, I had to get to her. I stepped out into the road, trying to force one to stop for me, but they just leaned harder on their horns and shouted at me to move out of the way. I called my driver, knowing he would be unable to reach me. Everything started spinning around me; the rising shouts, the blur of cars and people. And then, a taxi pulled up beside me.

'Sister, I know you,' the driver said. 'Where do you need to go?'

I pulled open the door to the back seat and jumped inside, still dialling Horya's number. Finally, her voice came through on the line. I could barely hear her over the shouting around me, and around her.

'I'm near Chaman-e Huzuri,' she told me. 'I'm standing underneath a billboard.'

I cannot remember how long the drive took, nor what

the driver and I talked about, nor even the details of his face. It's strange, how little I can remember about one of the people who helped me most in those frantic last days. I have no idea why he stopped, or how he recognised me. I wonder whether he knows that he might have saved my sister's life.

When we found her, she was laughing. Brave, foolhardy Horya.

'I could have walked home,' she said as she clambered into the back seat beside me.

Of course, she had never known firsthand what life under the Taliban is like. Bravery comes easily to the ignorant. But despite her tough act I saw that her hands were shaking, too. The square near the university was even more packed than the streets around the defence ministry, and tense fear had boiled over into panic.

I still hadn't been able to reach Bashir. I tried to reason with myself that he, too, was in a noisy street where he couldn't hear his phone. Yet I also couldn't shake the gnawing thought that he might be in danger. Then, suddenly, he was calling me. Relief flooded over me as I heard his voice. 'Where are you?' he asked. He had been working in his office in the culture ministry when an assistant came to order him home. He had been experiencing the same set of emotions as I had: denial, anger, acceptance, panic. He was out on the street, trying to find a way through the mess. I told the driver where he was and we set off towards him.

Through the car window, I watched as my city morphed before my eyes. Just yesterday it had been the same old Kabul, a joyous, scruffy city creeping up into the mountains that cradle it. I always felt as if I knew every single one of its four million inhabitants. On the pavement outside the gaudy green and orange awning of the Barg Continental, one of the most popular restaurants in the city, the street children would try out their salesmanship.

'Aunty, you promised last time that you would buy some!' one of them always said as he proffered his strips of chewing gum to me. I would take a couple to reward him for his chutzpah. The smells of the streets were so familiar, a comforting air of grilling meat and vegetables, mixed with the smoke of the charcoal they were cooked on. It was a big city, and yet it often felt like an extension of my family home.

That day, the city had palpably changed. Expressions I had not seen before crept across people's faces. It set off the fear in me. The shopkeepers were pulling iron shutters down over their windows. The street vendors were turning off their griddles.

'Oh, my god, they've broken the jail! All the prisoners are out!' a woman screamed.

Another was collapsed on the pavement, crying. 'My god, my husband! What will I do?'

I looked over at Horya, who was staring out of the window on her side of the car, watching a different version of the same scene play out. And then it hit me, my fear like a muscle memory from two decades earlier kicking in: we were two single women, travelling in a car with a man who was not our relative. And the rules of our city had changed.

I began frantically calling Bashir, until finally he answered. He told us which direction he would be walking. We found him after forty minutes, pushing his way through the crowded streets that had turned into a scene from a disaster film. The taxi driver couldn't take us any further: the roads were now so clogged that no cars were moving at all, and he had his own family to get back to. He refused to be paid. So we hopped out, and the three of us started struggling through the throng. I clung onto Bashir's hand and Horya clung to mine, and like that we made it to a shop that was still open. Horya could get away with her outfit if we ran into the Taliban, but I might as well have been wearing a sign on my head: *I am a government worker.* In Kabul I wore tailored trouser suits, which until today had felt like armour, a crisp professional exterior with which I could take on any challenge my job threw at me. Now my clothes left me exposed. I needed a new camouflage.

The shopkeeper we found had not allowed a crisis to get in the way of good business. Amid the rising horror on the streets outside, he had spotted an opportunity for profit. He had almost sold out of long dresses; clearly I wasn't the first woman to run through his doors in a panic that day. 'Two thousand five hundred Afghani,' he said. I almost swore. He was asking for more than twice the normal price, weighing how much money he could make against how soon the Taliban might arrive and perhaps extort some of that profit from him. On a normal day, I would never have bowed to this. Today I had little choice. Cursing, I handed it over.

Cheaply made and synthetic, the dress was not good value. I began to sweat and stumble, unaccustomed to the baggy folds catching around my heels. Soon, my feet were bleeding, the straps of my shoes cutting into the flesh.

But we kept walking, kept pushing, until we reached my mother's home.

It had only been six hours since I last saw her, but my mother understood the new rules. She was stuffing everything that had belonged to my father, all his uniforms and military mementos, into a bag, and was searching for a place to hide it. My sixteen-year-old sister Marina was lying pale and red-eyed on the floor.

'If they come I'll throw myself out of the window,' she said. 'I'd rather die than live under their control.'

How I wanted to stay there and comfort her, and help my mother sweep the house clean of our past. I wanted to lock the doors and close the shutters, and then curl up with my siblings on the sofa, singing to them or watching a film. But my presence there was putting them in more danger, and the knowledge of it chewed away at me. Five minutes after I had walked in the door, Bashir and I were leaving again, forcing our way back into the crowds. The midday sun scorched the crown of my head through my scarf, and I had not even thought to change my shoes.

By the time we reached my apartment in north Kabul, Taliban fighters were moving into the street behind my building. I peeked over my balcony wall and saw their flag flying from a new checkpoint below. We had minutes to get everything and leave before they started knocking on doors. I swept my photographs, my documents and some clothes into a bag, and Bashir and I ran down the stairs and out to the street.

'Hurry up, come on, come on.'

I don't know why, but I took the time to lock the door

before I left, and then stowed the keys carefully in my pocket. The new furniture I had bought, the delicate lace curtains over the windows, our books, the flat-screen TV – I had resigned myself to losing it all. But when I came to my white wedding dress, I sobbed. I had to make a choice: I could take it with me, or my father's military uniform. I knew straight away what it would be – I could not leave this last memento of my dad to the Taliban. But leaving the wedding dress left me distraught: I could barely let go of it, despite the precious minutes ticking by. It was not about how much money it cost, nor the fact that I was unlikely to find another one the same. It was because it was one of the last things my father saw. He had been telling everyone that I would look like an angel in it.

I ran down the apartment entrance steps and bundled myself and my belongings into the car. The sound of a doorbell playing 'Happy Birthday' rang out down the deserted street.

Kabul was shutting its doors on me. The places I could go were dwindling. The same went for Bashir – the Taliban knew him, too. My friend Tamana, a filmmaker who was in enough trouble herself, had come to pick us up from my apartment; she was one of the few people we knew who still had access to a car. As she drove us away from my neighbourhood we debated frantically about where we should go. Suddenly Tamana banged the steering wheel and whooped, one of our few moments of genuine happiness that day. She had thought of a place. It was an apartment in a part of the city I had never been to, one of the pricey new developments with underground parking and security gates that had been built for foreign aid workers and local elites. I kept my headscarf low on my forehead and tried to look as casual as possible as the gate swung open. Inside, I sat on the balcony listening to distant gunfire and opened my Facebook for the first time in days.

The situation in Kabul was far worse than I had thought. The small snapshots of pandemonium that I had witnessed were microcosms of the entire city's collapse. Bashir deleted posts and pictures until his thumbs ached, purging anything that might give our location away. I tried to help, but found myself transfixed by the videos. The government had buckled, despite the president's pledges that it would fight on. There was no central authority, no law enforcement. Taliban militants were entering the city with zero resistance and now they were set on revenge. Already, there were some unconfirmed reports, reposted by my friends, of human rights activists being arrested.

I clicked through the grainy clips, my mouth dry. At the airport perimeter, huge crowds were trying to push their way through the gates, only to be pushed back by shouting American soldiers and beaten by prowling Taliban fighters. In the city centre, grinning jihadis were riding their motorbikes down streets where Kabul's elites had been shopping and dining a day earlier. Friends wrote that the Taliban had started going door-to-door, searching for wanted people. And then, the worst video of all. Crowds had managed to force their way into the airport, overwhelming the soldiers at the gate. Once inside, they had flocked to the runway, desperate to board a flight to anywhere. Men and boys ran alongside a huge military plane as it taxied for take-off, gripping any part they could. As the plane lifted into the air, the bodies began to fall.

I could not stop replaying it, even though my chest tightened more each time I did. I wondered what those men had been thinking in their final moments as their grip on the landing gear loosened. Did they really think they would be able to cling on for hours, in freezing temperatures at high altitude? What did they think would happen when they landed? Did they know that they would die, and did they care?

On the second night of the Taliban takeover, a message pinged onto my phone from friends in the United States. I was to go to the airport the next day. They had arranged permission for me and my family to leave on an evacuation flight, an increasingly rare ticket out. As soon as the sun came up, Bashir and I drove to my mother's house. Eight of us piled into a car that was designed to carry five, me sitting on the floor covered with bags in case we passed any Taliban checkpoints. I began to believe that things were going to be OK.

In recent years, Kabul airport had been improving. The last time I had gone through, in July 2021, on my way back from Dubai, I was impressed: there was a small café selling teas and snacks and a new check-in area with ropes strung between gold posts to mark out the queues. The road outside was newly paved and free of litter, and inside there was a roomy departure lounge with comfy seats. The upgrades had been long overdue. Foreign money had been flowing into Afghanistan for twenty years; some of it had to find its way down to the people. It's not like Kabul was still a backwater – aid workers, diplomats, journalists, even some tourists were flying in and out all the time. But even before it was 'done up', there was something about it that I loved.

The dissonance between my last memory of the airport and what we found there that day was one of the hardest things for me to process about those surreal final days in Kabul. I heard the cries as we pulled near the airport, terrified yelps and screams. When I poked my head out of the car door I saw pandemonium: the crowd running towards us, away from the gate. Beyond the mass of bodies, I heard shooting. The Taliban had set up checkpoints around the perimeter of the airport, and they had opened fire on the people trying to get inside.

My sisters and my mother were screaming. For ten seconds I was transfixed, staring at the wide eyes of those running towards us. Then, my instincts kicked back in.

'We need to get out!' I shouted, and pushed my little brother back into the car. Once we were all inside the driver shot backwards, turned sharply and sped away. On the short drive back to my mother's house everything that had gone right on the way there went wrong. The Taliban was tightening its hold on Kabul by the minute, and streets that had been safe an hour earlier were death traps. We got stuck in the gummed-up traffic, next to a pick-up truck full of Taliban fighters. They were pointing their Kalashnikovs at people, barking orders down at them. Terrified, I cowered lower into the footwell.

In the slice of the outside world that I could still glimpse through the bags and the bodies surrounding me, I watched a scene play out that will stick in my mind for ever. A column of US and Afghan National Army vehicles was passing over the crossroads in front of us, one of a thousand small retreats underway across Kabul. They were heading towards the airport, to secure the last space in the city they still held. The Taliban fighters were holding the traffic back to allow them to cross, and they were jeering: 'Congratulations on the victory!' and waving their white flags triumphantly. The Afghan soldiers did nothing. That day, for the first time, I was glad that my dad was no longer alive. It would have killed a piece of his soul to see that.

That same day, the Taliban held their first news conference. How different their face was for the TV cameras compared to the streets. Zabihullah Mujahid, their spokesman, promised they would show respect for women's rights, put a stop to the crime and insecurity that had plagued the country, and rebuild the economy.

'We want to assure the residents of Kabul of their full security ... the protection of their dignity and security and safety,' he said.

Tell that to the people being beaten at the airport gates, the women being hunted down in their homes, and the boys and men falling to their deaths from the landing gear of a plane.

Three days later we tried again. Things had grown worse in the interlude. The crowds at the airport gate had thickened and the people had become more desperate. The Taliban was securing its hold on the city street by street. My friend's apartment was no longer safe, so all of us had piled into the home of my mother's uncle, in a poor district close to the airport. With the curtains drawn and the door locked, we fixated on our social media feeds to keep up with what was happening. Our group grew. People were calling, asking if they could come with us. Bashir's friend came to us with nothing but the clothes he was wearing: he had left all his documents behind, scared that if he was found with them by the Taliban, he would disappear. My mum's cousin, a doctor who had been working with foreign donors, asked us to take him, too. This time, the car meant for five carried eleven. Again, I lay in the footwell covered in bags. By now, the streets were riddled with checkpoints. Every time we went through one, I stifled my sobs, and held my breath.

Our flight was due to take off in the evening, and we were told to go to the airport in the morning and wait. But there were no instructions for how we could get to the gate. The streets surrounding the airport were thick with humanity: there were thousands of people, not the merest space in between them. The air was heavy with the smell of toilets and sweat. Nobody would give an inch for anyone else to push through. Everyone was shouting at the soldiers who were guarding the gate.

'I'm a British citizen!' I heard one man shout.

'Please, I'm a mayor!' shouted another.

The soldiers at the gate looked scared. They were pushing people back and raising their weapons. 'Get back!' they shouted. 'Don't come! Go away!'

I managed to push my way through to the front and held up the US visas that had been emailed to me, but the tall American soldier didn't care. To him, I was just another shouting face. 'Wait over there!' he ordered. And when I looked, I saw he was pointing to the area outside the gate, where thousands of others were also standing.

The heat of the day was building and bearing down on me. The stress and the noise were inflicting a physical ache. I bought a bottle of water from a small boy beside me and quickly dipped my face mask to take a swig. A few seconds was all it took: I heard a man murmur next to me: 'She's the mayor!'

This was what I had feared. The Taliban were at the airport gates now, just metres away from us. If one person told them who I was, they could snatch me and I might never be seen again. I pretended I hadn't heard, and backed away.

Moments later, someone tapped me urgently on the shoulder. 'There's a back way in!'

He whispered that there was a secret entrance, that we should go down an alley to the side of the airport and we would find it. But when we started in the direction he had pointed, something about that alley chilled me. It was narrow, with the high razor-wired wall of the airport on one side and the rough walls of a slum district on the other. The road was unpaved, and dusty. At the other end I could see that it opened out into a green area with trees, but after just a few steps my stomach felt as though it was filling with wasps.

'We can't go down here,' I said. 'There's something wrong.'

I heard a shout from behind us. It was Bashir's friend, waving wildly to stop us.

'There are Taliban at the other end!' he cried.

It was a trap. Taliban spies had spotted me and tried to

lure me to a place where they could capture me. That last-minute instinct had saved me.

We had to get inside the airport. My gut feeling told me that if we did not manage to leave today, we never would. I pushed back through to the gate entrance with my family linking hands in a chain behind me. By now our names were on evacuation lists with the US, UK, Spain and Germany, too. But a sudden glimpse of a Turkish flag on the uniform of one of the soldiers at the gate sparked an idea. The Turkish deputy ambassador to Kabul was a friend, and had told me a day earlier that if I needed help at the airport gate I should call him. I had to dial several times because signals were jammed but eventually I got through. He told me to send him all of our names and passport details and we would be allowed through. After everything, it was that easy.

A Turkish soldier opened the gate. I pulled my family through, at the same time feeling terrible for the strangers that crowded around us.

'Please, take us with you!' one woman shouted.

'We have passports! We have visas!' begged a man.

It was only when the gate had slammed behind us that I realised that Roman, my fourteen-year-old brother, was not with us. He had been at the end of our chain, and at the last moment his grip on my sister's hand had slipped.

I turned back to the soldier. 'Please, my brother's still out there!'

It could have been five minutes that I was searching for Roman, or it could have been five hours. I just remember a blur of faces and my frenzied shouts. What if he had stumbled and people were stepping on top of him? What if he had been pulled away by a Taliban spy? In a string of terrible moments, this was the worst. When I spotted him he was just ten metres from the gate but jammed between bigger bodies. Nobody would give him an inch. Shouting at the men to move out of the way I forced myself to him and grabbed hold of his hand.

Three cars were waiting for us inside the airport gate. In the back seat, my sisters and I sat in silence for the first time since that morning. It was Marina who broke first.

'Look at us!' she cried. 'Look at what we've become.'

I held her head to my shoulder, trying to absorb her grief. She shook with sobs, inconsolable. My mother was next. When we poured out of the cars into the military terminal at the far end of the airport, tears started leaking from her eyes, too. The staff from the Turkish embassy brought us food: ice cream, chocolate, pasta, food you would eat at a family celebration.

In my head I was already making plans. I would find my family a place on an evacuation flight and then I would leave them, go back out the airport gate and home to my apartment, and carry on with my work. I could survive if it was just me. It was my family who had to get out. I turned to my mother and told her. Her eyes filled again.

'I've already lost my husband. I cannot lose you, too,' she said.

The belly of the plane gaped open, its stark light glaring onto the runway in the blackness. A silent line of people shuffled forward.

Bashir took my hand and pulled gently. 'Come on, we have to go.'

I was stuck, rooted to the ground as if I was tethered. I tried to lift my foot and break my inertia, but I could not budge. Desperate to hold onto the last moments before I boarded, I reached down and scooped up a handful of earth, knotting it into a corner of my scarf.

'Come on!'

A fresh relay of gunfire – staccato, insistent – started up beyond the airport's perimeter fence: *Rap. Rap-rap-rap-rap-rap.* Tracer bullets arched like dancing fireflies under the starlight. Bashir pulled my hand again, harder now, and I jolted forward, joining the column sliding into the plane.

Inside, we sank into a space on the floor. We were surrounded by blank expressions and wet eyes, and engulfed by a low hum of endearments over stifled sobs. Keepsakes spilled out of grubby knapsacks. School certificates. Baby shoes. In my fingers I clutched the black folder that carried photographs of my engagement. I hardly recognised my face from that day, when it was dramatically made up with white skin and pink lipstick to match my embroidered silk dress. It stared back at me, alien and smiling; the me of two years ago a stranger.

The injustice of it all. For my mother, for whom this was just the latest in a lifetime of losses. For my brothers and sisters, who had been told that they were inheriting a better Afghanistan. For Bashir, who had spent fourteen years serving his people and country. For the other families around us, some of whom had been at the airport for days. And for me. How hard I had worked, how hard I had struggled, and suddenly none of it counted. None of this was our fault, I thought. We were not the ones who engineered this failure, yet we were the ones who were paying. We still did not know where we were going. We did not know who else might make it out of Kabul. We did not know if we would ever be able to return. In my last moments on the soil of my homeland, I sang a song of exile, its lyrics a testament to Afghanistan's pain:

> *I have become homeless*
> *I have moved from one home to another*
> *Without you, I have always been with sorrow, shoulder*
>   *to shoulder*
> *My only love, my existence*
> *My poems and songs have no meaning without you*
> *My land*

Nine

February 2022

Kabul

The convoy of pristine white Toyotas barged their way through gridlocked streets, horns blaring, until they reached the fortified entrance of the Serena Hotel. The traffic backed up behind them as the security guards – Taliban soldiers – checked the vehicles and waved them through.

Inside, the Serena was the same as it had always been. The lobby was delicately scented and soft music played in the background, and the staff were dressed in immaculate uniforms that nodded to traditional Afghan costumes. Scruffy journalists slouched on the sofas and suited diplomats hurried through. In this luxury fortress, business carried on as normal; it was as if the regime had never changed in Kabul. The sole sign of difference was the delegation of Taliban dignitaries who had arrived in the convoy, and who were now gathered in the lobby, shaking hands and kissing each other's cheeks. But for their turbans and beards, they could have been officials from Ashraf Ghani's government; they, too, had met in the best places in town.

When I arrived in Kabul a week earlier, my first emotion was gut-twisting fear, tinged with joy. Soon after our escape from Afghanistan my family and I had been offered asylum in Germany, in the same small town my aunt lived in. We were settled in two clean and modern apartments, one for Bashir and me, the other for my mother and siblings. The thick silence and calm on the German streets was a relief at first. I knew we were lucky to have been given a new home so quickly, but my mind and heart were still in Kabul. I followed each small development there on Facebook and Twitter, more engaged with the screen than with the world around me. When bombs exploded outside Kabul airport, killing scores of those still trying to get onto evacuation flights, I collapsed against a wall and wept.

It was on Facebook that I learned about a woman in Ghazni province, south of Kabul, who was trying to sell her daughter. The girl, thirteen years old, was the youngest of four, and her mother was a widow. All of her children were girls, which was considered shameful for her husband while he had still been alive. Now they offered her an earning potential. With the fall of the country to the Taliban, almost all the international aid organisations had pulled out their teams, and then crushing sanctions were slapped down, plunging the country into poverty; however, since the Taliban's return she had been unable to beg on the streets, much less go out to find work. She was asking for 2,000 euros for the girl. Instead of seeing all her children starve, the woman had decided it would be best to send one of them to another house, and bring in money to keep the rest of them alive. I asked one of my friends who was still in Afghanistan to track the woman down, and I began to collect donations for her, starting at the conference in Switzerland where I was giving a speech that week. Bashir and I both cried as I asked everyone in the hall to contribute money for the woman to save her daughter, partly from shame: we never expected to find ourselves in a place where we had to beg for money from people in a foreign country to save Afghan children. We were able to give the woman 1,000 euros – enough to keep her daughter at home. Knowing that one girl had been saved gave me a brief buzz of happiness.

So I channelled my anger and sadness into activism. I found a speaking agent, and started talking at events all over Europe, trying to keep the humanitarian and political crisis in Afghanistan on the international agenda, even as it was overtaken by other events. Angela Merkel, one of my political heroes, invited me to a private audience with her. Politicians and celebrities wanted to have their picture taken with me, and journalists begged for my story. I posted daily on Twitter, amplifying news of the Taliban's crackdown on women's rights activists who had remained in Kabul. With the money I earned from speaking and awards of cash prizes, I rebooted my humanitarian organisation, Assistance and Promotion for Afghan Women (APAW). I had been unable to continue working on it when I became mayor, but kept it ticking over as a brand. With the help of colleagues and my maternal uncle

Haji Muma, I had opened an educational and vocational training centre and a maternity centre in Kabul. I was now able to provide food packages to the very poorest women, mostly widows who had no income. Haji Muma sent regular updates, including photos that I would linger over, wondering what else I could do.

But nothing could fill the aching hollow in my chest, or hold back the primal urge to get back home. In Germany we sank into a bleak, grey winter. The last heat of the summer sun disappeared almost as soon as we arrived, replaced by a chilly monochrome. The leaves fell from the trees I had so admired in early autumn, and for months the sun barely broke through the clouds. I lost weight, and my hair started falling out. I saw strands every time I looked at the floor, triggering my old compulsive disorder that I inherited from my dad. The only sounds from the desolate streets were church bells and occasional sirens. To the locals I was just another refugee, someone to be pitied or perhaps despised. I saw it in people's faces as I sat on the bus on my way to appointments at the job centre and my German language classes. I felt that they looked at my headscarf and came up with stereotypes: *Muslim woman, oppressed.*

If only they knew what I had done in my homeland. How I had the courage to stand apart from my society, my colleagues, my family. How the work I did there made a difference, however small, to the lives of the people I encountered. Most of all, how I longed to go back.

I started thinking about returning to Afghanistan from the moment I landed in Germany. At first it was a vague wish, like something a child might ask the tooth fairy to grant. I wanted to go to Surobi and eat fish, or take a boat out on the reservoir at Qargha. When a few airlines started resuming flights to Kabul my daydreams sharpened into the beginnings of a plan.

In early February, I approached the German foreign ministry to ask if they would help me coordinate a short visit to carry out humanitarian work, that perhaps I could use my profile partly as a means of protection. They immediately responded, saying they would inform the Taliban leadership that the German government's cooperation with humanitarian assistance to Afghanistan would depend on my safety. The last step was to get my own assurance from the Taliban that I would not be arrested as soon as I arrived. I did not want to negotiate with them, nor meet with them in Kabul and be used by them as a photo opportunity to convince the world that they were treating women well. I knew that I was walking a thin line, and that many people would criticise my decision. But I had to have that assurance.

'Afghanistan is your home and no one can take it away from you,' said Zabihullah Mujahid, the Taliban's spokesman, when I called him to tell him of my plan. 'Whenever you want to come back, you have the right.'

I told only Bashir that I was going. He pleaded with me not to but when he realised I was determined, he initially said he would go with me. I said no, that I was terrified for his safety, and that if anything happened to me it would be better if he were in Germany, working our contacts to get me to safety. At the airport, we both cried as we said goodbye. Three times I walked through the sliding doors of the airport entrance and turned back, to see Bashir still standing in the same place, red-eyed.

The flight stopped over in Dubai, and as I waited there

to board the Kam Air flight to Kabul, I studied the faces of my fellow passengers, sure that some were staring at me a little too hard. In the air, I steeled myself for the reactions I might face on the ground. But when I first saw the mountains of Kabul through the window, the snow gleaming under the sun that I had yearned for during the dreary, dark months in Germany, I forgot all my fears. Whatever the politics, and whoever was in charge, Afghanistan would always be my home.

Once we landed, and were inside the terminal, I realised that many of the people on my flight were just as apprehensive as I was. In the passport queue, most of them were speaking English, even though I knew they were Afghans; in a strange flip of fortunes, having a connection to a foreign country was now a measure of protection. My first sight of the Taliban came as I put my bags through the scanner at the airport's exit. When I picked the bags up on the other side, I came face to face with two of them, just a metre away and sizing me up from behind a glass screen. For a moment I wondered whether the assurances I had been given were a lie: if I had walked into a trap, and was now going to be led directly into prison. The burlier of the two, dressed in camouflage and with a thick brown beard, locked his eyes onto me. His stare, unfriendly and enquiring, reminded me that it doesn't matter how brave you are in such moments; your fate is entirely dependent on the mood of that one person. After five long seconds, the Talib turned to his colleague and started chatting. I hadn't realised, but I had been holding my breath. Now I exhaled, long and slowly; I was of no interest to them at all.

*

The Afghan tricolours that had flown above the airport terminal had been replaced with the Taliban's banner, a white flag inscribed with an Islamic incantation written in black Arabic script: *There is no God but God*. On the street, vendors who had once sold trinkets printed with Ashraf Ghani or Hamid Karzai's face had switched seamlessly to selling wares advertising the Taliban. There were checkpoints everywhere; as spring approached, the new rulers were bracing for attacks. They had quashed the resistance quickly in August 2021, but the rival mujahideen factions were now regrouping, spurred on by opposition leaders outside the country who were calling for an armed uprising. The opposition strongholds, such as they remained, were in the Panjshir valley north of Kabul, where the Tajik warlord Ahmad Shah Masood is still deified. Each night, the Taliban carried out security operations, going through Kabul district by district, searching every family home for weapons. The visa queue outside the Iranian embassy stretched hundreds of metres down the street, a line of people desperate to leave before the country descended into civil war yet again.

Aesthetically much was the same, however. The advertisements for gyms still featured muscular, bare-chested men flexing their arms, and there were still women on the streets, some of them even showing flashes of glamorous outfits beneath the long shawls they covered themselves with. Younger girls carried schoolbooks. There were still dozens of murals of the Afghan flag painted onto the blast walls, even though the Taliban's white flag now flew over the roundabouts. Graffiti must have been low on their priority list. Drug abuse, though, was at the top. Close to the Pol-e Sohkta bridge, I spotted a Taliban round-up of opium addicts, all of them thin and dejected. They would be shipped off to the Taliban's new rehabilitation centre on the city's outskirts – no luxury place for sure, but more than the old government had offered. The Taliban were even letting journalists in to film it. At the checkpoints, the Talibs were wearing matching uniforms so clean they could have been national army soldiers. They had a patch with a logo, a black scorpion on a red background, and wore US commando-style sunglasses. As I approached the first one after leaving the airport I sank down into the back seat of the car, and pulled my face mask higher. Yet after a brief glance inside, the soldier waved us off with a thank you. The old government's soldiers had generally been rude and aggressive to civilians going through checkpoints. None of them had ever said thank you.

The dissonance threw me, more so than the terror I had been expecting. All my life, the Taliban had been the thing I feared most, the entity that inhabited my nightmares and caused so much of my trauma. I hated it. Taliban fighters had killed my dad, forced me to give up being mayor, and finally to flee. They preached a form of Islam that was alien to me, and since they had retaken control of Afghanistan they had persecuted their opponents, including female activists, several of whom had been imprisoned and killed. Yet here was Kabul, still functioning, in some ways more efficiently than it had before.

The old government had been corrupt and dysfunctional; I regretted the time I had worked for them in the ministry of defence. Even though I had been doing my best to help war widows, I felt that I was still part of a bad system that was rewarding some parts of the country and ignoring the rest. Meanwhile, in the villages, the Taliban gained support by creeping into the places the government ignored. I was not able to speak out against the injustices and ineptitudes I saw; the way the war widows' pensions were so patchily distributed, and how the national army soldiers had been left on the frontlines of the battles against the Taliban with almost zero support.

So now, if women were still on the streets, and if there was peace in the country, and nobody was being forced into following reams of petty rules, then was this Taliban worse only in different ways than those who had been in power before? If so, then what did the battles I had been fighting my whole life mean?

I found the real blowback of the past six months on the outskirts of the city, in Dasht-e Barchi, a poor district mostly inhabited by ethnic Hazara. Here, the snow had been cleared into pebbly heaps by the roadside and then blackened by the diesel fumes. Standing amid the grime were hundreds of people, offering up paltry wares: thin mattresses, rusted kettles, and bags of used clothes – mean household possessions they were trying to barter for a few hundred Afghani.

The sanctions and the end of aid operations were having an effect on the Afghan people that was far worse than the simple fact of Taliban rule. Poverty has always been searing in my country, but now an international freeze on Afghanistan's assets meant that the new government could no longer afford to pay the wages of state workers. The little money left in the coffers was being creamed off by the Taliban and its supporters, of course. Meanwhile the middle classes – teachers, nurses, and other professionals who had been surviving under the old government – were also plunged into poverty. I knew this in theory, since I had been working on establishing my humanitarian project in Germany. But it was a shock to see it in front of me.

In Dasht-e Barchi, in a yard where chopped wood was stored under tarpaulin, a group of local women was waiting for me. I had asked the elders of the neighbourhood to invite the poorest women, so that they might receive an aid handout of rice, flour, sugar, oil and tea that would keep a household sustained for a month. Before the distribution, I sat with them and asked about their lives. All were widows, apart from two who were disabled.

'I don't have anyone to support me, and no opportunity to work,' one told me, the others telling similar versions. This wasn't something new that had started with the Taliban – it had been the problem in Afghanistan for decades. Women were infantilised, told they were only capable of bearing children and looking after the house. Yet at the same time, the men were slaughtering each other, leaving those women to fend for themselves while they lacked the skills to do so.

As I talked with the women, dozens of men gathered around the fringes, goggle-eyed and still gripping the wheelbarrows they had brought to collect their wood. Now, one of them piped up.

'Why is this aid only for women?' he demanded. 'Men need help, too. We have to work and support all the family. Why isn't this aid coming to us? I have seven children!'

I have never backed down from debates like this. I thrive

on them. I walked over to where the men were standing, and stood open-armed in front of all of them.

'OK, so why did you have so many kids if you aren't able to look after them?' I asked the man. 'And do you also allow your wife to work, to bring in some extra money?'

For a moment he was taken aback, not because he was ashamed of his choices, but because these were options he had never considered.

'But women aren't strong enough to work!' he retorted.

I turned to the women, who were sitting patiently waiting for their packages. They had watched the whole scene with a bemused sense of despair.

'What do you think, sisters? Are you strong enough to work?' I asked them.

One of the oldest caught my eye, and raised her eyebrow. 'That guy wouldn't even be here if a woman hadn't been strong enough to give birth to him,' she sighed.

Talking with women of my grandmothers' generation enthrals me; I see them as portals to a time when Afghanistan was at peace, and our society was strong. Those of my mother's generation tell stories I can relate to: they lived through all the shifts and conflicts that have beset Afghanistan since the 1970s. Before my father died, I never considered my work as activism: I was a politician, doing my job. But when I lost him, the trauma rewired my brain. In those early months after his murder I would talk without stopping for hours; someone might ask me what I had eaten for dinner and I would answer by talking about food and then go off on tangents about Afghanistan's troubles. So I know that, sometimes, all that someone needs is a person who will listen. We sat together on hunks of chopped wood, the spring sunshine on our faces as we talked about the people we had lost – husbands, fathers, brothers and sons. And as the women poured out their stories, their pain and their hopes, I could almost see their burdens lifting. I might have been giving them food to survive, but emotionally, they gave me far more than I gave them.

It was only hours after I had posted pictures of the aid distribution on social media that the reactions started rolling in. By the evening, there were almost a thousand comments on my Twitter post. Many of them were positive, expressing surprise that I had returned but gratitude that I had. Others were less complimentary.

'All your life you've just been trying to make the Hazara happy,' wrote one.

'She's Pashtun, that's why she's able to go back,' wrote another. 'She has obviously made a deal with the Taliban.'

Meanwhile, Taliban supporters accused me of having a hidden agenda.

'She's doing this as a project for foreign governments,' wrote one. 'She's establishing another foreign project.'

Another suggested I should be tracked down and killed.

These comments did not really bother me. The ones that did came from other women's rights activists who were mostly in exile and infuriated that I had come back. They accused me of whitewashing the Taliban, making it seem as if all was fine for women in Afghanistan, and that I was causing major damage to our cause.

'You must explain what your deal was with the Taliban,' wrote one, 'so that we can do the same.'

Some said this proved that I had fabricated the Taliban attacks on me, and the murder of my father. None of them seemed to realise or acknowledge the personal risk I had taken. A couple of days into my trip, when I was just beginning to release the tension I had held in my body since leaving Germany, one of the young Talibs manning the checkpoints decided to wield some authority. There were five of us in the car, with two men in front. I was in the back with another woman and a young Hazara man called Aman who had come to the aid distribution. The Talib shot one look at Aman and demanded to see his papers. Was he these women's *mahrem* – the official guardian that must accompany a woman according to the strictest versions of Islam? Aman admitted that he was not. The soldier ordered him to get in the front with the other men, meaning he had to perch on the knee of the man in the passenger seat for the rest of the journey while we women sat in roomy comfort in the back. To this Talib, apparently, that was more acceptable.

I can find black comedy in the moment now but, in different circumstances, and had there not been foreigners in the car, Aman would almost certainly have been hauled off and beaten, and perhaps me, too. I dug my nails into my palms while we were at that checkpoint, not daring to hope that we would come away free and unscathed. Throughout my life, whenever I have seen something improper, I have always spoken up: I physically cannot stay silent. But in that moment I had to, for the good of everyone in the car, and it scorched my conscience. I admit it: before that one scrawny guy at that unimportant checkpoint, I had started to hope, against all the world leaders and the international opinion, there might be something left in Afghanistan that I could work with. I was never naïve enough to think that the Taliban would offer women equal power and a voice, nor that the sanctions would be lifted and life could carry on as before. But in the few days that I had spent in Afghanistan to that point I had begun to tentatively dream about what I might be able to do – perhaps to return again and expand my aid project, carry on showing my face in Kabul to let everyone in Afghanistan know that women cannot be silenced there. Now I had to wake up and realise that I was in a system where anyone could do anything to anyone. Those female activists in Taliban prisons? Some of them must have been dragged there because of random bad luck at checkpoints. As we drove away the silence burned in my throat. I longed to scream out and declaim the injustice of which that young Talib was proof. He did the worst thing to me – he took away my hope.

I hadn't told my maternal family that I was coming to Kabul. They still lived in a block of flats in the Arzan-Qemat district of Kabul, my grandmother on the top floor and my uncles and their families below. It took several rings of the doorbell to get anyone to answer. Eventually some of my little cousins ran out to the balcony and shrieked with delighted surprise when they saw me waving from the pavement below.

'Go and get Bobo Jan!' I shouted up.

My grandmother couldn't stop staring at me. It was as though a phantom had appeared before her eyes.

'Just this morning your cousin's brother asked me to sew something for him, but I told him that among my grandchildren it's Krishma who deserves everything, and see now you are here!' she laughed.

My maternal family never call me Zarifa – instead, they use my nickname, Krish, a shortened form of Krishma, which means affection. I had two personalities as a child: sweet one moment and fiery the next, and over the decades my two names were the means by which my family came to accept my choices. The woman out there bossing men around? That's Zarifa, with her armour of three tough syllables. The girl they know at home, soft and nurturing? That's Krish.

My uncle Haji Muma, my mother's eldest brother, has always loved me as Zarifa. He is a bear of a man, with thick grey hair and beard and a wide, gleaming smile. He has a cosmopolitan sense of style, wearing velvet jackets he buys from London over his Afghan shalwar khameez, and he speaks English with delightful imperfections, having worked with foreign aid organisations. Haji Muma was part of the delegation who persuaded my father to let me go to India. Now, he was doing all the field work for my charity.

My younger uncle's construction firm had won huge contracts with the former government just before it was toppled, but was forced to stop his projects midway through when the Taliban took over. He had no way of knowing if they would ever see the promised return on the hundreds of thousands of dollars invested.

Both my uncles hated the Taliban. This was the house where we stayed in the middle of our chaotic two-day effort to get out of Afghanistan in August 2021. When they waved us off that final morning, they did not know if we would fall into the hands of the Taliban, or return from the airport, unsuccessful, or if we would find our way onto a plane and fly away, returning who knows when.

Now, my uncles and I were trying to see our way in the same Taliban twilight zone.

'For sure there are Talibs doing bad things,' said Haji Muma. 'But we're most afraid of a war in Kabul. Afghans are hopeless now. We spent twenty years building something up, and in one moment everything was destroyed.'

That night the Taliban were conducting their security sweep in the next neighbourhood down from my grandmother's. The following evening they would be at her house, polite but quietly threatening as they checked IDs and searched for weapons. Yet at the same time, the security situation in Afghanistan had suddenly brightened, since Afghans had stopped killing Afghans. Women were in the bazaars, and Kabul University had just reopened with a part of the campus set apart for women.

'If we had foreign support, this regime would be better than the Ghani government,' Haji Muma said. 'Politics is like a game. Only the regime has changed, the people have not.'

If he had told me this three days earlier, when I was still in Germany, I would have accused him of being brainwashed, or suspected that he was speaking under duress. But now that I was in Afghanistan myself, I was beginning to understand how, for the people still living there, this repressive peace was preferable to the violent freedom they had enjoyed, or endured, for twenty years. It is very easy to call for revolution when you are an activist outside the country, with the luxury of not having to live amid the blowback. Yet one thing played on my mind, stirring the uneasy feeling that still nestled in my gut: the only thing you could not do, Haji Muma said, was criticise the Taliban.

I had in my mind an idea of what my aid centre might be like through the pictures Haji Muma had sent me. I knew that with the money I had sent to him he would use all his aid work experience to make something good. I had told him what I wanted to do in Afghanistan, about the plan that had been forming inside my head from the moment I arrived in Germany. I would not be working in politics again, at least not in an official way. And I could not be an activist sitting in Germany, shouting from afar. I knew I had to get back to the people, to my people.

Aid is not just about distributing packages. It is also about helping others – in my case other women – learn how to generate an income for their lifetime. Haji Muma and I brainstormed ideas. Tailoring and making handicrafts were the easiest options, we decided. A woman didn't have to be literate to sew beautifully and be creative with her work, and people always need clothes. And what could the Taliban find immoral in a room full of women with sewing machines?

In the flesh, our project was so well turned-out that I gasped when I walked inside. Haji Muma had chosen the location well: also in the Arzan-Qemat district, close to the family home, tucked away discreetly on a busy road with no signs to give it away, and where a small compound was hidden behind iron gates. In a basement room that was nonetheless bright and well-organised, an instructor called Mareena taught a classful of young women how to sew on basic, hand-cranked machines. I went round the room, greeting them one by one, and they paused working on the infant romper suits they were making, showing me their progress. The seamstress-teacher Mareena, a middle-aged woman wearing a full face-covering niqab, had been widowed eight years earlier, yet thanks to her work she had been able to support her children through university. The girls had been selected by the elders in their neighbourhoods, who had heard announcements about our project in the local mosques.

I asked the girls if they were enjoying their course.

'Of course!' one sweet-faced teenager replied. 'Before I was just sitting at home doing nothing.'

'Now I can sew clothes for my children,' another woman said.

Across a small courtyard, we had set up a maternity clinic and pharmacy, offering free care and medicines to our students. For non-students, we offered pre-natal check-ups at a fraction of the price of most hospitals – 60 Afghani compared to 400 elsewhere in Kabul. Our doctor, Paimana Jan, told us that eight women had been to the centre that day alone, for ultrasounds and blood tests, and had been prescribed medicines at a 40 per cent discount from normal prices. For the births, however, they would still have to go to hospital, though there had been an exodus of doctors since the Taliban takeover. Doctor Paimana reckoned that one obstetrician was covering for four that had left.

'They left. They're gone now,' she said. 'I don't think we'll ever know why. We're here to serve the nation and the country. We should stay. If everyone decided to leave, who'd take care of those left behind?'

I asked her if she was pleased to see me back in Kabul.

'Yes,' she said, and my heart skipped upwards, glad of the affirmation after the trolling on social media. 'Everyone is leaving,' she continued. 'But you are back, and you are helping.'

My interview with 1TV, Afghanistan's biggest private television channel, was recorded on my last evening in Kabul, to be broadcast as I was mid-air on the flight out. Despite the storm whipped up by my first social media posts, I kept tweeting and posting on Facebook and Twitter every day, highlighting my project and, more importantly, the humanitarian crisis. Not only did I attract controversial responses, I also immediately attracted the attention of the media. A young female journalist from Pazhwak TV arrived as I was distributing aid to the Hazara women in Dasht-e Barchi, and then TOLO, one of the most critical opposition channels, also asked for an interview. I bumped into foreign journalists on assignment in Kabul, some of whom had met me when I was mayor of Wardak, and so I did interviews with the French, Spanish and Swiss media. They all wanted to know the same thing: why was I back? And what was I going to do next?

I swerved the political questions in those early interviews, batting off the implications that I had come back through an agreement with the Taliban.

'Whether I come in or out is no one's business,' I said to one of the journalists. 'I have the freedom to decide that. I'm here for the welfare of my people.'

But for the last interview, which would be the main story on 1TV's 8 p.m. news bulletin, the most talked-about political programme in the country, I decided to be more candid. 1TV had been forced off air when the Taliban took control but it began broadcasting again on YouTube, from a new headquarters in Germany. My interview, recorded in Kabul, would be my one chance to reveal what had been playing on my mind.

The 1TV interviewer asked me if I had any criticisms of the Taliban.

I did.

'The Taliban,' I began, 'need to immediately release all female prisoners. Those who have fought for women's rights, in the service of a better Afghanistan for everyone, should not be in a prison cell.'

Though it was never stated explicitly that I shouldn't criticise the Taliban, and in fact Mujahid had said I could say whatever I wanted, I knew that it was dangerous to do so. But to come back to Afghanistan and be only a few miles or even metres away from the women in jail, and not say anything about their nightmare? That was not just unthinkable to me – it was unacceptable. I would say my piece in the interview, weigh up the reaction from the safety of Germany, and decide later if another trip back to Afghanistan would be possible.

But even if I hadn't done the interview, and said what I did, a return was not assured. The Taliban were behaving well now, but that was because they had things to gain. They wanted to take up Afghanistan's seat at the United Nations, and have the burden of sanctions lifted. They were stating publicly that they would respect women's rights, and allow girls to return to schools and universities. But the behaviour I witnessed and the facts I knew proved that behind the public face, there were many angry young men who believed now to be their time for revenge. Give it another six months, a year, as the world grew distracted by other disasters, and the Taliban could easily slip back into their old groove, particularly if a new civil war broke out. They had promised to allow girls to return to school, but when it came to the first day of term, the girls were blocked at the school gates and left in tears. The Taliban had done exactly the same thing in the nineties, leaving my generation of Afghan girls to learn the alphabet in dank basements. As I had seen at that checkpoint in Kabul, this was a regime that could never be trusted to keep its word.

Even so, I spent my last night in Afghanistan elated and proud at having had the courage to come back and look them in the eye. I couldn't wait to hug Bashir again on my return.

The young man behind the counter scrutinised my passport, and then my face.

'You're the mayor, aren't you?' he asked. 'Aren't you blacklisted?'

Then, a moment later: 'Stand over there.'

He beckoned a group of men from an office. They were Taliban, and they did not want to let me leave Afghanistan.

'Where is your *mahrem*?' a tall one in a brown turban and shalwar khameez demanded. 'You can't leave the country unaccompanied.'

There was an hour to go before my flight departed. My interview would be shown three hours later, and there were no other flights until the next day. The Talibs had taken my passport and German residency permit, and were now looking through my phone. But it was anger, not fear, that boiled over in me.

'You killed my *mahrem*!' I shouted back. 'And my other *mahrem* is in Germany, and you would probably take him hostage if he came here. So what should we do? Will one of you marry me and be my *mahrem*?'

They turned away and snickered, like schoolboys. My heart thumped back down to my stomach. I knew in that moment that they were not going to stop me from getting on the flight: they just wanted to use what power they had to scare me. I started going through my phone, trying to get through to my contacts in the German foreign ministry. None of them answered. I had quick, tense calls with the team I had been travelling with in Kabul, who were not able to get into the fortified airport without tickets of their own. I called Bashir, whose stricken voice pained me more than my own situation.

I could hear them muttering a few metres away from me. 'She used to talk so badly about us, and look at her now!' said one.

Eventually, the head of the gang came back to me. 'The problem is, you've been insulting the Islamic emirate,' he said. 'That is not acceptable. But we are letting you leave the country. Go on. Get out.'

There were now thirty minutes until my flight departed. I still had to get through a final security check before I could board. But I could not waste this opportunity.

'You need to learn how to speak respectfully to women!' I said, drawing myself up to my full height, still only coming up to their shoulders. 'It is a shame for you to take pictures of my passport and residency, and look through my phone.'

They listened with a cold detachment. I knew very well that this was just a cruel trick done by sadistic men, and that they didn't have any real power over me. I also sensed they had done this before. An airport worker, a civilian who was directing passengers into the passport queues, kept trying to catch my attention and gesture how sorry he was. I could see tears had gathered in his eyes as the Taliban bullies stood over me. A couple of times, when I was sitting and waiting for them to make a decision, he came close enough to whisper a few words.

'I'm so sorry this is happening to you,' he told me. 'So many of us are proud of you.'

My generation of Afghan women inherited nothing, and much of what we gained was taken from us. What we have left is now in the hands of a group we remember and fear. The rights that women still enjoy in Afghanistan – to go to school, to walk on the streets, to get a job – are bestowed on us by the Taliban, even as they lock up the women who have been fighting and striving for those things for years. We are allowed to have this much, but we must never threaten to ask for more.

The Taliban are a fact. No foreign army is coming to boot them out again, and the armed resistance is too weak to overthrow them. We know too that the Taliban are not inclined to treat women well, whatever mask they might momentarily wear. But if I can still find or create even the smallest space under the Taliban regime where women can learn, work and give birth safely, if not freely, then I must continue to help.

Though some might say that what I am doing damages our cause, I ask – which war are Afghans really fighting? To many Afghan activists outside the country, resistance means terror and guns. They say that this is the right resistance, to risk everything in pursuit of total glory. But Afghan men fought the Soviets, then fought each other, then fought the Americans and then each other again. As women, we have suffered men's slaughter for generations. My grandmother was a widow at twenty-seven; my mother was fatherless at three and a widow herself forty years later; I myself bear the weight of my father's murder.

Sometimes you don't need to die with a gun, or win all your battles at once. You just need to put your fears and politeness aside, come out of your house, take courage, and push back the boundaries, little by little. Women around the world and throughout the ages have forced change from their spaces out, through education, trades unions, charitable organisations, and through often heroic lobbying – squeezing every bit of advantage from their positions, however small – in total and together; and however slowly and carefully, they created change.

The Taliban say they are now more enlightened than they were in the 1990s. This is because they have been forced to be: for twenty years, my Afghan sisters and I have been devouring the opportunities presented to us to become doctors, supreme court judges, journalists – and mayors. Millions of us have learned to read and write, the first step to taking control over our lives. A young Kabul generation with no memory of the mujahideen's civil war, we mingled in the coffee shops and accepted each other, Pashtun, Hazara and others alike. We helped to change our society in those two decades, and as a result the Taliban was compelled to reform.

You do not have to negotiate with the Taliban to talk to them. You do not have to cut deals or make bargains to listen to them, and present your ideas. It is easy for journalists and diplomats to speak with members of the leadership council. Those are the polished guys, of course, who have reached their positions through diplomacy and wit. They might just be a smooth front, but if I can talk to them, human to human, Afghan to Afghan, it is possible for me to influence their thinking. If I can go to places like Changa, and ask the villagers why they support the Taliban, it is the first step to finding new ways to challenge their beliefs, and present them with options. I am prepared to speak with those I dislike and distrust, or whose ideas differ from mine, if it means that I carry on with my work. Better that than to shout from afar. I have the time and patience to continue this struggle, speaking with women one at a time, exchanging ideas and planting new seeds. Let official Afghan politics carry on without me. I am happy where I am, for now, and I am free.

What is more, I know we will win, eventually, because women can no longer be ignored in Afghanistan. Girls like me found a window of opportunity and we clung onto it: schools, university, jobs outside the home. We were able to do that because of our mothers' determination that we – their daughters – would not have our intelligence go to waste, as theirs had. It is our responsibility now to keep that window open, push it wider, and invite more women – and men – to do the same. I will keep talking to the people of my country, despite our differences, because our traumatic history connects us all. I will keep reminding women that they have a voice, and can raise it. And that is why I fight on.

Acknowledgements

Thanks and respect to my parents and dear family, who were always by my side, supported me in every way, and despite all the good and bad around my life, they still gave me a reason to continue fighting for what I believe in.

I would like to extend my thanks to all those people who have helped me to tell my story: my agents, Kelly Falconer and Oliver Stoldt, for their enthusiasm and encouragement, and my editors around the world, in particular Rose Tomaszewska, Anupama Roy-Chaudhury, Clive Priddle and Katharina Festner for their belief.

To Marcel Mettelsiefen, for sticking with me through the good times and the bad, and for capturing parts of my personality that no one else tried to find.

To Hannah Lucinda Smith for being my bestie, and more than a friend now.

Finally, thanks to the Times Digital Archive, for helping me to piece together my memories.

Zarifa Ghafari is an Afghan activist, politician, and entrepreneur. In November 2019, she became the mayor of Maidan Shahr, the capital city of the Wardak Province, Afghanistan. She is one of the only female mayors in Afghan history and the youngest – appointed at age 26.

As mayor, Zarifa became a role model to women in Afghanistan. She introduced an anti-litter campaign and made a special appeal to the US Secretary of State, Mike Pompeo, to safeguard women's rights following the uncertainties posed by the Taliban USA negotiations. In 2020, Zarifa was chosen as an International Woman of Courage by the US Secretary of State.

Hannah Lucinda Smith is the author of *Erdogan Rising: The Battle for the Soul of Turkey* (HarperCollins/William Collins 2019) and is the *Times* correspondent in Turkey, where she has covered conflicts, a coup attempt, and the rise of controversial president Recep Tayyip Erdogan. During her time in the region, she has also reported on the Middle East, from inside rebel-held Syria and on the front lines of the battle against Isis in Iraq, and joined the mass movement of migrants on their journey to Europe in 2015. She has also worked for the BBC, contributed to the *Atlantic* and the *Spectator*, and been awarded a Pulitzer grant to write for *Wired* magazine.

PublicAffairs is a publishing house founded in 1997. It is a tribute to the standards, values, and flair of three persons who have served as mentors to countless reporters, writers, editors, and book people of all kinds, including me.

I. F. STONE, proprietor of *I. F. Stone's Weekly*, combined a commitment to the First Amendment with entrepreneurial zeal and reporting skill and became one of the great independent journalists in American history. At the age of eighty, Izzy published *The Trial of Socrates*, which was a national bestseller. He wrote the book after he taught himself ancient Greek.

BENJAMIN C. BRADLEE was for nearly thirty years the charismatic editorial leader of *The Washington Post*. It was Ben who gave the *Post* the range and courage to pursue such historic issues as Watergate. He supported his reporters with a tenacity that made them fearless and it is no accident that so many became authors of influential, best-selling books.

ROBERT L. BERNSTEIN, the chief executive of Random House for more than a quarter century, guided one of the nation's premier publishing houses. Bob was personally responsible for many books of political dissent and argument that challenged tyranny around the globe. He is also the founder and longtime chair of Human Rights Watch, one of the most respected human rights organizations in the world.

· · ·

For fifty years, the banner of Public Affairs Press was carried by its owner Morris B. Schnapper, who published Gandhi, Nasser, Toynbee, Truman, and about 1,500 other authors. In 1983, Schnapper was described by *The Washington Post* as "a redoubtable gadfly." His legacy will endure in the books to come.

Peter Osnos, *Founder*